Income Inequality

Income Inequality

Why It Matters and Why Most
Economists Didn't Notice

MATTHEW P. DRENNAN

Yale UNIVERSITY PRESS
New Haven & London

Yale University Press books may be purchased in quantity for educational,
business, or promotional use. For information, please e-mail
sales.press@yale.edu (U.S. office) or sales@yaleup.co.uk (U.K. office).

Set in Minion type by Integrated Publishing Solutions.
Printed in the United States of America.

Library of Congress Control Number: 2015940164
ISBN 978-0-300-20958-7 (cloth : alk. paper)

A catalogue record for this book is available from the British Library.

This paper meets the requirements of ANSI/NISO Z39.48-1992
(Permanence of Paper).

10 9 8 7 6 5 4 3 2 1

To my wife, Katherine Van Wezel Stone,
My children, Matthew, Maureen, and Erica,
And my grandchildren, Grace and Ava Drennan

Contents

Acknowledgments

This work has been more than four years in the making. It began as an insight in early 2009, in the wake of the initial shock of the financial crash, when I realized that the dramatically rising income inequality of the past three decades might have played a role. The more I explored the data and the debates about causes of the crash and ensuing Great Recession, the more convinced I became that the conventional economic explanations were missing a critical piece of the puzzle. I realized then that it was necessary not only to put income inequality back into the story but also to explain why that part of the story had not been told already. That is, I wanted to understand why economists had failed to see the significance of the most important economic trend of the past three decades—the dramatic rise in inequality.

Many institutions and people have assisted in this work. The Russell Sage Foundation generously financed the first phase of this study. In addition, Cornell University's Podell Emeriti Award for Research and Scholarship provided subsequent funding for research expenses. From the beginning of this project, the Luskin School's Department of Urban Planning at the University of California, Los Angeles, provided the library resources, an office, IT assistance, and most im-

portantly, colleagues, which are so necessary for academic research. For the semester that I spent in New York City, I was
generously provided with an office at the New York University
Schack Institute of Real Estate by the dean, Rosemary Scanlon,
and a professor there, Hugh Kelly.

UCLA's statistical consulting group at the Institute for
Digital Research and Education gave me invaluable assistance
at every step. I sent them countless email queries that they an-
swered in a day or less—right answers, too. I made many trips
to their walk-in consulting sessions, trips that were always
worthwhile.

I had the good fortune of having a number of astute, sup-
portive, yet critical readers. I particularly want to thank Alan
Altshuler, Charles Brecher, Robert Hockett, Raymond Horton,
Morton Horwitz, Christopher Jencks, and David Rigby for
pushing me to sharpen my arguments and sharing with me important literature. I also want to thank participants in the Brown
Bag Lunch speaker series at the New York Federal Reserve Bank,
where I made an invited presentation on this project in the fall of
2012. Among the participants, Erica Groshen, Andrew Haughwout, and James Orr offered cogent remarks, and they pointed
me to important data sources. Two anonymous referees de-
serve thanks for suggestions that markedly improved this
manuscript.

I have had the great benefit of the services of several tal-
ented graduate students at UCLA. The spare simplicity and
clarity of the tables and figures I attribute to two excellent research assistants at UCLA: Anne Brown and Taner Osman.
They both know that the sole purpose of tables and figures is
to elucidate the argument, not to drown it in obscurity. Of the
nineteen tables, Anne produced sixteen of them, and I did the
other three (Tables 4.4, 4.8, and 4.11). Of the thirteen figures,

Anne produced seven (Figures 2.1, 2.2, 4.1, 4.4, 6.1, 6.2, and 6.4) and Taner produced five (4.3, 5.1, 5.2, 5.3, and 6.3). One figure, 4.2, is taken from an International Monetary Fund (IMF) paper with permission. Anne Brown has been a critical assistant in the final preparation of the manuscript to Yale's exacting standards. Mike Manville, a former Ph.D. student in urban planning at UCLA (now an assistant professor at Cornell), read every word of various drafts in the early stage of producing this book. He made both substantive and technical suggestions that I mostly accepted.

I wish to acknowledge my editors at Yale University Press, William Frucht and Jaya Chatterjee, who have made this book production process exciting rather than tedious. My copy editor, Joyce Ippolito, and my production editor, Ann-Marie Imbornoni, purged the manuscript and proofs of numerous flaws I had overlooked, and they did that with speed and grace. Their standards of excellence and respectful treatment would flatter any author.

Most of all I thank my wife, Katherine Stone, who encouraged me in pursuing this project from the beginning and discussed the ideas in depth. She also read every word more than once, and her suggestions have enhanced the final manuscript. She has been an invaluable asset for my project, always eager to help and always giving excellent suggestions.

I

Introduction

This book tells two stories. The first tells how rising income inequality over the past decades led to rising, indeed surging, household debt to support consumption, a surge that brought on the financial crisis and Great Recession of 2008–09. The second shows that mainstream economists have adhered to a theory of consumption that assigns no role to the distribution of income, and therefore is inadequate for fully understanding the Great Recession or preventing the next one.

Of course rising income inequality is only one of the causes of the surge in household debt, but it is an important one that is too often neglected by economists and policy makers. The period from about 1995 to 2007, especially post 2000, can be characterized as a perfect firestorm of household indebtedness, fueled by four factors: (1) stagnant incomes for most households related to the long-term rise in income inequality; (2) unusually low interest rates after 2000; (3) legal and institutional changes that relaxed borrowing standards of lenders, raised the availability of credit, and made housing a more liquid asset; and (4) the housing price bubble. The bursting of that bubble in 2006–07 precipitated the financial crisis and the Great Recession, but it was only the last straw. The debt-supported expansion of consumption became unsustainable after 2007. Because consumers have begun to reduce their debt—deleveraging—and increase their saving, consumption will be depressed for some years, producing an anemic recovery.

Most analyses of the financial crash and Great Recession identify factors (2) through (4) as causes but not (1), income inequality. Some, such as Till van Treeck, identify (1), rising income inequality, as well.

> There is substantial evidence that the rising interhousehold inequality in the United States has importantly contributed to the fall in the personal saving rate and the rise in personal debt (and a higher labour supply). Aided by the easy availability of credit, lower and middle income households attempted to keep up with the higher consumption levels of top income households. This has contributed to the emergence of a credit bubble which eventually burst and triggered the Great Recession.[1]

The evidence that lower- and middle-income households were trying to keep up with the consumption of top-income households is less substantial than the evidence that they sought to maintain their living standards in the face of stagnant or declining incomes.[2] Joseph Stiglitz, Raghuram Rajan, Paul Krugman, and Thomas Palley also name rising income inequality as a cause of the jump of indebtedness and ensuing economic crash.[3] Two writers go further, linking inequality to the stagnant economic recovery from the Great Recession.[4] They all make well-reasoned arguments linking growing personal indebtedness in part to rising income inequality, but fail to provide empirical support for such a link.

This book goes beyond their writings in three ways. First, it presents econometric evidence supporting such a link. Second, it uses household budget data to show that households' increased indebtedness was not merely for leisure or competitive conspicuous consumption. Rather, the drivers of debt were increased spending on what most would agree are necessities. Spending on shelter, health, and education has increased significantly despite stagnant incomes. In other words, with stagnant or declining incomes, households maintained their consumption on essentials through massive borrowing. And finally, it presents persuasive historical evidence that the nation has been through this before—this is not the first time that rising income inequality accompanied by growing and unsustainable household debt and the bursting of a real estate bubble ended in a severe economic crash.

Why did most economists fail to see this problem coming? The inclusion of rising income inequality as one of the four major causes of the financial crash and Great Recession does not comport with the mainstream economic theory of consumption. Indeed the econometric evidence, the household budget evidence, and the historical evidence argue that the mainstream theory of consumption, which posits no role for income inequality in the economy, is seriously flawed. The story here is that increasing consumer indebtedness, which supported consumption until the crash in 2008–09, was driven by the pressure for most households to maintain consumption in the face of stagnant income as income inequality relentlessly rose for thirty years or so. That debt-supported expansion of consumption became unsustainable after 2007 once house prices tumbled.

Economists have ignored or misunderstood the effects of rising income inequality on macroeconomic outcomes. Moreover, the mainstream consumption theories cannot explain recent trends in relative consumption and saving. Neither Milton Friedman nor Franco Modigliani and Richard Brumberg—the leading theorists of consumption in recent economic thought—posited any role for the distribution of income in their theories of consumption. Friedman's permanent income theory of consumption does not explain the observed rise of debt-fueled consumption in the decade before the crash. Modigliani and Brumberg's life cycle theory of consumption contains the seed of an explanation, but not one that they anticipated.

However, if we look further back in time, Thomas Malthus, writing in the early nineteenth century, had the germ of an idea that excess saving, brought on by a top-heavy distribution of income, would curb effective demand and thus crimp the expansion of total output. But Malthus had no data, and his prose was less than lucid. A century later, Keynes picked up on Malthus's idea, which had lain dormant thanks to the triumph of David Ricardo's general equilibrium perspective on the macro economy. Some of Malthus's thinking on effective demand is echoed in John Maynard Keynes's *General Theory of Employment, Interest, and Money* (1936).

Keynes's theory of consumption, fully developed in the *General Theory* and translated into algebra by his interpreters, dominated macroeconomics for many years. It attributed an important role for income distribution in macroeconomic outcomes—namely, that the share of all households' after-tax income spent on consumption, the average propensity to consume (APC), would decline over time as incomes rose, curbing effective demand and perhaps leading to long-term stagnation. But the post–World War II experience contradicted his inference. The APC did not decline; it was either stable or rising. So the Keynesian notion that a more equal distribution of income would curb the fall of the APC disappeared, and income distribution no longer mattered for the theory of consumption.

Around 1985, however, something strange began. After a long period of stability, as hypothesized by Friedman as well as Modigliani and Brumberg, the APC began a long-term *rise.* That meant a long-term fall in the saving rate for the same period because the saving rate is equal to (1 – APC). That event was not supposed to happen in Friedman's theory.

Was the observed rise of the APC, 1984–2005, unprecedented? No. Based on Simon Kuznets's data, there was a forty-year rise of the APC, 1894–1903 to 1924–33. Kuznets's data on income distribution, which begins in 1920 and ends in 1938, shows rising income inequality in the 1920s. The fact that Kuznets's long period of rising APC includes a decade of rising income inequality, and that the thirty-eight-year rise of income inequality, 1974–2012, includes a long period of rising APC, raises the question of whether there is a causal link from rising income inequality to rising APC.

The mainstream consumption theory of Friedman as well as Modigliani and Brumberg cannot explain such a link. Instead, faced with slow or no income growth, households might resort to increased borrowing to maintain some desired level of consumption. The demand for borrowing can be curbed by interest rates and a hard income constraint. But in the period from about 1995 to 2007, especially post 2000, there was an unusually huge rise in household indebtedness, fueled by the four factors noted above.

This book does not address the question of how to fix rising income inequality through public policy. However, it does address the possible causes of rising inequality.

As to policies to redress rising income inequality, some authors have recommendations that would be moves in the right direction. They include reducing the amount of money in political campaigns and lobbying, and enforcing the labor laws and the antitrust laws on the books. But any effort to redress income inequality must begin with a story about why curbing and reversing income inequality matters for the long-term health of the economy. That is the central goal of this book.

The book will begin by briefly laying out the facts about rising income inequality, a topic that has been exhaustively covered elsewhere.[5] Income inequality has been rising for almost four decades. Median incomes and wages have stagnated, while the share of income going to the top 1 percent has soared. We will list and evaluate the possible causes of rising income inequality, and then examine the large rise in consumer indebtedness post 1995. The rise of debt and income inequality has been accompanied by a measured increase in economic insecurity among consumers. Also, relative spending on housing, health, and education has risen markedly, squeezing relative spending on other necessities, so we will see some reasons why income inequality matters. Turning to economic theory, the book traces the treatment of income distribution, or lack thereof, in theories of consumption from Malthus, Ricardo, and Keynes to Friedman, Modigliani, and Brumberg, to modern critics of mainstream neoclassical consumption theory, including behavioral economists. The dominance of Friedman's as well as Modigliani and Brumberg's theories of consumption among macroeconomists up to the present explains why most, but not all, economists have not noticed that income inequality matters. Then we present an outline for a revised theory of consumption that fits the facts. As we will see, the rising inequality and debt leading up to the Great Recession matches a similar trend that preceded the Great Depression.

II

Trends in Income Distribution

The changing distribution of income in the United States has some distinguishing characteristics. The first is that the share of national income going to labor has been declining. Splitting labor income between the share going to the top 1 percent of wage, salary, and bonus earners and the bottom 99 percent shows that the top share is rising. Trends in productivity, hourly earnings, male and female, as well as all household income show shifts favoring the highest income groups.

It is important to explain what income inequality means, what it is and what it is not. If the proportion (share) of aggregate income received by the lower end of the income distribution is falling over time, *that* is rising income inequality. But how is "lower" defined—99 percent, 95 percent, 90 percent? An easier rule of thumb is that if the Gini coefficient or the Theil index is rising over time, *that* is rising income inequality.

Rising income inequality does not necessarily mean stagnant real incomes for most households. During the Depression years, the nation had stagnant incomes for most households but *falling* income inequality. From 1947 through 1973 the nation had rapidly growing incomes for most households and also had falling income inequality. And in the decades leading up to the financial crash and Great Recession, the nation had stagnant income growth for most households ("stagnant" here is defined as real mean income growth of less than 1 percent per year) and rising income inequality. The point is that the two factors—rising income inequality and stagnant household income growth—do not necessarily always occur together. Indeed, although the data are murky, household income was likely growing from 1890 to 1914 and income inequality was rising. In what follows, most of the evidence is about the decades preceding the financial crash, when both rising income inequality and stagnant income growth for most households occurred together. That was not a coincidence. The strong growth of aggregate income, 1947–73, was cut almost in half in the recent period, 1973–2007. At the same time, the share of income going to the top 10 percent rose from 32 to 46 percent. Slower growth plus a declining share for the bottom 90 percent meant that average real income of that group did not rise. Of course, it rose strongly for the top 10 percent.[1]

Labor's Declining Share of National Income

One of the regularities noted in the past about the United States economy was the long-run stability of the shares of national income paid out to labor and to owners of capital—two-thirds to labor and one-third to capital.[2] Table 2.1 presents the share to all labor for the years 1969 to 2013. The share barely changed in the twenty years from 1969 to 1989: 65.0 percent to 65.2 percent. But then it began to edge downward, falling to 60.7 percent by 2013.

Table 2.1. Labor Share
of National Income,
1969–2013

Year	All Earnings
1969	65.0%
1979	66.6%
1989	65.2%
1999	64.1%
2007	63.4%
2013	60.7%

Source: Bureau of Economic Analysis
(n.d.), Table 1.12.

The decline in labor's share of national income is not limited to the United States, but is seen in other rich countries, as noted by Peter Orzsag.[3] He calculates that the drop of five percentage points of labor's share of private sector income from 1990 to 2011 is equivalent to a loss of $500 billion. He attributes the drop in share to technological change and globalization. Joseph Stiglitz does not agree. About the declining wage share, Stiglitz noted, "The pattern and magnitude of changes in labor compensation as a share of national income are hard to reconcile with any theory that relies *solely* on conventional economic factors."[4] And further, "If technological change increases the effective supply of labor, and labor and capital are not very substitutable, then technological change drives down the share of labor. But the pattern of increase of wages—with wages at the very top (e.g., of bankers) increasing so much relative to that of others—is consistent with the view that something else besides technological change is causing the decline in the wage share."[5]

**Table 2.2. Shares of Earnings to Top
1 Percent and 99 Percent, 1929–2011**

Year	Top 1 Percent	99 Percent
1929	8.7%	91.3%
1969	5.2%	94.8%
1979	6.2%	93.8%
1989	8.7%	91.3%
1999	11.7%	88.3%
2007	12.2%	87.8%
2011	11.0%	89.0%

Source: Based on Saez (2013), Table B2.

The Rise of the 1 Percent Among Wage Earners

There is a long-standing popular perception that the rich get their income from ownership of capital, while workers get their income from wages and salaries. This was roughly true during the roaring 1920s, but it is not true any longer. Based on income tax data, the top 1 percent of tax filers for 1929 received 29 percent of their income from wages. But in more recent years, their share from wages (which includes bonuses) has ranged from 54 to 66 percent.[6] It is still certainly the case that most capital income accrues to the 1 percent, but they, mostly managerial and professional workers, are receiving an increasing share of all earnings.[7] Table 2.2 shows the shares of total wage income for the top 1 percent and the other 99 percent for selected years, 1929 to 2011. The two shares sum to 100 percent, of course. The share of the top 1 percent moves down from 9 percent of all earnings in 1929 to 5 percent in 1969. Thereafter their share rises to 12 percent in 2007 and drops to 11 percent by 2011 with the onset of the Great Recession. The 1 percent's gain in share since 1969 mirrors the 99 percent's drop in share.

Productivity, Hourly and Annual Earnings, and Rising Income Inequality

It is a fundamental truth of economics that living standards can rise in the long run only if productivity rises. Although that condition is necessary, it is not sufficient. Compensation must rise in tandem with productivity growth for living standards to improve. Figure 2.1 shows the trends of real hourly compensation and productivity (real output per hour worked) for the United States for the post–World War II period. The two measures rise together until the 1970s, and then diverge. Growth of compensation no longer keeps up with growth of productivity.

But the average growth rates conceal how the productivity gains have been distributed. In an analysis of Internal Revenue Service (IRS) data examining productivity growth, the authors conclude, "Our most surprising result from the large IRS data set is that, over the entire period 1966–2001, *only the top 10 percent of the income distribution enjoyed a growth rate of total real income (excluding capital gains) equal to or above the average rate of economy-wide productivity growth.* The bottom 90 percent of the income distribution fell behind or were even left out of the productivity gains entirely."[8] This pattern of productivity growth outstripping wage growth over the past three decades is repeated for other rich nations.[9]

The drop in the earnings share of national income, the drop in the 99 percent's share of earnings, and the disconnect of hourly compensation growth from productivity growth all point to relative slowing in the growth of individuals' earnings.

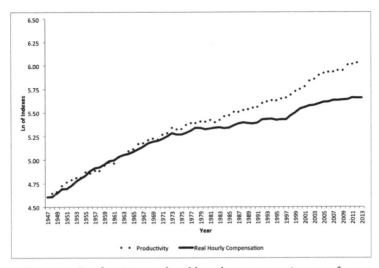

Figure 2.1. Productivity and real hourly compensation, nonfarm business sector, 1947 through first quarter 2012. *Source:* Bureau of Labor Statistics (2015).

Table 2.3 documents the slowdown of earnings growth. Panel A of Table 2.3 shows trends in median real earnings, male and female, of full-time year-round workers. The median real wage for males increased about $7,000 in the seven years from 1967 (the first year of the Current Population Survey income data) to 1974 (the year after which income inequality began to rise). However, in the thirty-three years from 1974 to 2007, that wage barely changed. The median for females grew more than the male median in both periods, but it also slowed markedly in the long period, 1974–2007.

It is clear that growth of real wages was either stagnant (for females, 0.9 percent per year) or almost nonexistent (for males, 0.1 percent per year). Some observers have argued that the massive rise of women in the labor force post 1970 was in

Table 2.3. Summary of Real Earnings and Income Trends, 1967–2013

| | 1967 | 1974 | 2007 | 2013 | Average annual percent change | | |
					1967–74	1974–2007	2007–13
Panel A. Median real earnings of full-time year-round workers, 2013 $							
Male	43,796	50,540	50,684	50,033	2.1%	0.1%	−0.2%
Female	25,307	29,694	39,436	39,157	2.3%	0.9%	−0.1%
Panel B. Median household real income, 2013 $	43,558	47,702	56,436	51,939	1.3%	0.5%	−1.4%
Panel C. Mean household real income, 2013 $	48,717	55,784	75,957	72,641	2.0%	0.9%	−0.7%

Source: Median real earnings of full-time year-round workers from DeNavas-Walt and Proctor (2014), Table A-4. Median and mean household real income from Table A-1.

part a coping measure by households to deal with flat wages for men.[10] In Panel C of Table 2.3, median household income is compared with mean household income. Growth of both the median and mean slowed markedly during 1974–2007 compared with 1967–74.

None of the statistics presented so far measures income inequality directly. Rising income inequality means that the relative distribution of income from all sources—earnings, dividends, interest, rent, and transfer payments—becomes smaller for those at the lower end of the distribution and larger for those at the higher end of the distribution. There had been a long decline in income inequality, a rise in income equality, that was evident in the years after World War II. That decline began during the Depression of the 1930s and was accelerated by World War II.[11] The turnaround to rising income inequality occurred in the mid- to late 1970s. In Table 2.4, 1974 is the turnaround year, because after that date, the two measures of income inequality, the Gini coefficient and the Theil index, are always above their 1974 levels (for both measures, increases mean greater inequality and decreases mean less inequality).

Panel A of Table 2.4 presents percentage shares of aggregate income (before taxes) going to each quintile of households. Note that in the turnaround year of 1974 the relative distribution is quite similar to the 1967 distribution. Income inequality rose after 1974. Every quintile, except the highest income quintile, showed drops of share from 1974 to 2007. Loss of share for the bottom four quintiles continued through 2013.

Panel B of Table 2.4 shows mean household income by quintile in 2013 dollars for selected years, 1967–2013. The last column presents the average annual percentage changes in the means from 1974, the turnaround year, to 2007, the last year before the Great Recession began. All of the changes are

Table 2.4. Summary of Income Distribution Trends, 1967–2013

	1967	1974	2007	2013	Average annual percent change, 1974–2007
Panel A. Shares of household income of quintiles					
Lowest quintile	4.0%	4.3%	3.4%	3.2%	
Second quintile	10.8%	10.6%	8.7%	8.4%	
Third quintile	17.3%	17.0%	14.8%	14.4%	
Fourth quintile	24.2%	24.6%	23.4%	23.0%	
Highest quintile	43.6%	43.5%	49.7%	51.0%	
Panel B. Mean household income of quintiles, 2013 $					
Lowest quintile	9,615	11,685	12,792	11,651	0.3%
Second quintile	26,643	29,044	32,603	30,509	0.4%
Third quintile	42,540	46,811	55,344	52,322	0.5%
Fourth quintile	59,519	67,603	87,606	83,519	0.8%
Highest quintile	107,112	119,777	186,009	185,206	1.3%
Panel C. Measures of income inequality					
Gini Index	0.397	0.395	0.463	0.476	
Theil	0.287	0.267	0.391	0.415	
Panel D. Household income ratios					
90th percentile/10th percentile	9.23	8.58	11.18	12.10	
90th percentile/50th percentile	2.11	2.23	2.71	2.89	

Source: DeNavas-Walt and Proctor (2014), Tables A-2 and A-3.

positive, but they are quite dissimilar. Quintiles one through four grew less than 1 percent per year, defined here as stagnant growth. The top quintile grew more than 1 percent per year. Panel C lists the two measures of income inequality, the Gini index and the Theil, for the same years. In 1974 both the Gini index and the Theil were slightly lower than in 1967, indicating reduced income inequality. However, both are markedly higher in 2007 and in the last year, 2013.

Panel D shows the household income ratios of the 90th percentile (households in the top 90 percent of the income distribution) to the 10th and the 50th percentiles (households in the bottom 10 percent of the income distribution and households in the 50th percent). A rising ratio over time means that income growth in the 10th percentile is falling behind income growth in the 90th percentile. A falling ratio means the opposite. Note that the 90:10 ratio falls from 9.23 in 1967 to 8.58 in 1974, meaning that income growth was faster in the 10th percentile (the bottom group) than in the 90th percentile (the top group). That trend was reversed after 1974. In 2007 the ratio was 11.18, and it was still higher in 2013. The pattern is similar for the 90:50 ratio, although the rise after 1974 is less extreme.

The national trend of rising income inequality beginning in the mid-1970s is matched by a state trend of diverging wage growth beginning in the 1980s. The neoclassical model infers that wages in sub-parts of the nation will converge over time, as lower-wage labor moves to higher-wage areas, putting downward pressure on wages, and reduced labor supply in the low-wage areas puts upward pressure on wages. Historical data for states back to 1870 mostly support long-run convergence, except for the decades of the 1920s and the 1980s, but the divergence in the 1980s and the 1920s was dismissed by Robert Barro and Xavier Sala-i-Martin as aberrations at the time they wrote.[12] A more recent study using metropolitan areas instead of states found that the income divergence of the 1980s continued into the decade of the 1990s.[13] Thus *divergence* of income among cities and states may be replacing *convergence* of income argued by theory and mostly supported by the earlier data. What does this have to do with income inequality? If rising national income inequality is accompanied by divergence of income among parts of the nation, then regional divergence may be one source of the increase in national income inequality. James Galbraith provides recent striking examples of metropolitan areas surging way ahead of the pack in income levels.[14]

The survey-based Census data in Table 2.4 indicate that strong gains of income are concentrated in the top quintile or the top decile. The careful analysis of the long-term changing distribution of income, by Thomas Piketty, Emmanuel Saez, and their collaborators, is focused upon a breakdown of the top decile.[15] Their data, based on tax files rather than surveys, produces more accurate estimates of top income shares. Their data show that the gains in income share of the highest quintile illustrated in Table 2.4 are concentrated in the top 10 percent and especially the top 1 percent. Figure 2.2 shows the share of income received by the top 10 percent and top 1 percent from 1917 to 2012. The top 10 percent received over 32 percent of household income in 1974, a share hardly changed since 1947. But by 2012, the top 10 percent share was 47 percent. The top 1 percent fared even better, receiving 22 percent of household income in 2012, up from 8 percent in 1974.[16]

The sharp rise in income shares going to the top 10 percent and 1 percent post 1974 is not accounted for by renters. "The large shocks that capital owners experienced during the Great Depression and World War II seem to have had a per-

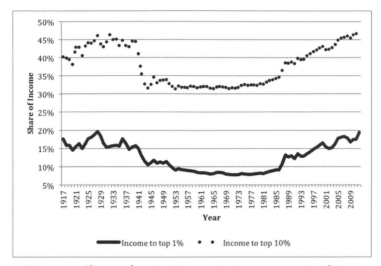

Figure 2.2. Shares of pre-tax income to top 10 percent and top 1 percent, excluding capital gains, 1917–2012. *Source:* Saez (2013).

manent effect: top capital incomes are still lower in the late 1990s than before World War I." On the other hand, they show that wage shares "were flat before World War II and dropped precipitously during the war. Top wage shares have started recovering from this shock only since the 1970s but are now higher than before World War II."[17]

III

Possible Causes of Rising Income Inequality

Why has income inequality been rising for almost forty years, as documented in Chapter II? There have been some excellent books and articles on causes of income inequality. They have one characteristic in common—they treat the major causes as political and institutional, not economic.[1]

This chapter is no exception. It weighs the evidence and passes tentative judgment. Of four broad categories of possible causes—economic, demographic, institutional, and political —the first two seem to be the least important.

Economic Causes

The view among most economists is that the pre-tax distribution of income is the result of market forces. The government amends the market outcome through taxes, transfers, and expenditures. Therefore, in the search for causes of rising income inequality among those who hold that belief, political causes are off the table. Among economists, the three most cited causes of rising income inequality are globalization, skill-biased technological change (SBTC), and job polarization. By globalization, they mean a number of factors that have become more important over the decades in the U.S. economy, including reduced trade barriers, increased immigration, lower international transport costs, off-shoring of production, foreign competition, and increased capital flows. In other words, U.S. labor is faced with more competition from foreign labor than in the past, because tariff barriers and transport cost barriers have diminished, making labor costs relatively more important. The increased off-shoring of production reflects the rise in importance of relative labor costs. Transport technology (container ships, super tankers, jet freight) and political agreements (the World Trade Organization, multi-nation trading blocs) have reduced transport costs and tariff barriers, making relative labor costs loom larger. It is not only goods production that has been off-shoring to nations with lower labor cost. Services such as call centers, routine legal and medical services, and software production have also shifted abroad, usually to English-speaking nations. The shift of services would not have been possible without the massive decline in cost and time of telecommunication services over the past fifty years. What does globalization have to do with rising income inequality? All of the factors noted put U.S. labor at a cost disadvantage with Asian, Latin American, and eastern European labor. U.S. wages will tend to rise more slowly than in the past before globalization. Most economics texts and media analysts treat globalization as the end of the story, but there is a problem in that analysis: Canada, the United Kingdom, France, Germany, and Japan are subject to the same forces of globalization as the United States. Have they had the same increases of income inequality? The United Kingdom and Canada have had increases, though less extreme than in the United States. Germany and Japan have had very little increases of inequality, and France has had none at all.[2] The comparison suggests that there is far more than globalization underlying the U.S. rise of income inequality.

Along with globalization, SBTC is another cause most cited by economists in explaining the rise of inequality. SBTC is defined as:

> a shift in the production technology that favours skilled over unskilled labour by increasing its relative productivity and, therefore, its relative demand. Traditionally, technical change is viewed as factor-neutral. However, recent technological change has been skill-biased. Theories and data suggest that new information technologies are complementary with skilled labour, at least in their adoption phase. Whether new capital complements skilled or unskilled labour may be determined endogenously by innovators' economic incentives shaped by relative prices, the size of the market, and institutions. The "factor bias" attribute puts technological change at the center of the income-distribution debate.[3]

Some examples can help here. In the past, the same workers who dug ditches with shovels could learn to operate a backhoe. The same workers who moved and stacked boxes in a warehouse could learn to operate a forklift. Productivity rose, but the labor skills required were not of a higher order. That has changed with the ubiquitous use of computers in factories, offices, and retail stores. There is a premium on information technology (IT) skills, often associated with college education. Even though the supply of college graduates has been expanding while the supply of high-school-only graduates has been shrinking, there has been a growing premium for the better educated. From 1979 to 2007 the median hourly wage of those with college degrees rose four times faster than the median hourly wage of those with only high school degrees.[4] This suggests that demand for highly educated workers has been outrunning the increasing supply.

One prominent economist who names SBTC as a chief cause of rising income inequality, even among the top 1 percent, is Gregory Mankiw. He claims that rising income inequality at the top is not because of politics or rent-seeking but rather supply and demand.[5] In other words, SBTC makes employers search out the best and brightest and reward them handsomely. Although one would think that SBTC does not affect incomes at the very top, some claim that SBTC affects pay of chief executive officers (CEOs), financial executives, attorneys, and athletes.[6] To place CEOs in the same category as athletes ignores the distinction between market and non-market forces. As Ian Dew-Becker and Robert Gordon have argued, "The core distinction is that superstars and other market-driven occupations have their incomes chosen by the market, whereas CEO compensation is chosen by their peers in a system that gives CEOs and their hand-picked boards of directors, rather than the market, control over top incomes."[7]

Piketty and Saez are critical of the SBTC explanation of rising income inequality. Wage shares in the United States, they argue, cannot be fully accounted for by skill-biased technological change, the favored explanation among economists. But for one of the same reasons globalization cannot fully explain rising income inequality in the United States, neither can SBTC. All industrialized nations experience SBTC, yet only the United States has had extreme increases of income inequality.[8]

Piketty and Saez are not alone in questioning the SBTC explanation for rising income inequality. Joseph Stiglitz notes, "Skill biased technological change has little to do with the enormous increases in wealth at the very top." Political scientists Jacob Hacker and Paul Pierson note that the rising inequality story is in the top 1 percent of households. They argue that education differences among workers and skill-biased technological change cannot fully explain the hyperconcentration of income at the top.[9]

There is no doubt that some of the rising inequality below the very top can be attributed to globalization and SBTC. But that cannot be the full story, because other rich, developed nations subject to the same forces have had more modest increases of inequality than the United States, and neither globalization nor SBTC can explain the huge gains of income share of the top 1 percent and 0.01 percent.

The third possible cause of rising income inequality developed by prominent labor economists is job polarization, "usually defined as stronger employment growth in jobs at the top and bottom of the wage distribution than in the middle."[10] Job polarization is commonly described as a "hollowing out" of middle-skill jobs. However, the job polarization model does not well describe changes in the labor market and link them to the rise of wage inequality. As Lawrence Mishel and his colleagues note, upgrading of occupations in the United States has been a long-term trend that can be traced back to 1950 with available data. Thus, it was occurring in the period of *falling* wage inequality, 1947–74, and in the period of *rising* wage inequality, in the late 1970s.[11]

In his recent book *Capital in the Twenty-first Century,*

Piketty identifies an economic cause of rising income inequality at the top. As the capital-income ratio slowly rises over time and the annual return to capital grows faster than gross domestic product (GDP), the share of national income going to the owners of capital rises, and so the share going to labor declines. The ownership of capital is highly concentrated among the top 1 percent of the income distribution, and so their share inexorably rises.[12] But that is a very long-term story and cannot fully account for the rising share of the top 1 percent documented in the previous chapter. It reflects the fact noted there that one-half to two-thirds of the income of the top 1 percent comes from earnings rather than capital. So Piketty's hypothesis, if true, would be a minor cause for the United States. Thus, to account more fully for the rise of income inequality requires looking beyond economic explanations.

Demographic Causes

The demographic portrait of the United States has undergone marked changes over the past thirty years or so. Some of those could raise income inequality. Married couples with young children have diminished as a share of all households, while single-person households have risen. The elderly population is growing rapidly as the baby boom generation moves into retirement. One of the most noted changes has been the increased labor force participation by women, which rose from 51 percent in 1979 to 58 percent in 2012.[13] One of the demographic changes that has raised income inequality is the tendency of highly educated employed females to marry males of the same status. In the 1950s, college-educated males who married were far more likely to have stay-at-home wives than today. A one-earner family back then with a college education had higher earnings on average than a one-earner family with high school only. Today, two-earner families, where both have college degrees, have far higher earnings than a one- or even two-earner family with high school degrees only. Thus they are further apart on the income distribution.

How much of the rise of income inequality could be explained by demographic shifts like the ones above? Rebecca Blank undertook a thorough examination of that issue in her book *Changing Inequality* (2011). Blank performs a number of careful simulations of effects on income distribution of various hypothesized demographic changes, such as: What if family type and size remained unchanged from 1979 to 2007? She finds, "In general, the results suggest that none of these changes, by themselves, would have major effects on income distribution. . . . Even large changes, however, leave income inequality closer to its 2007 level than its 1979 level, suggesting that a major reversal in inequality is unlikely in the absence of substantial and currently unforeseen changes."[14] Her rigorous analysis of demographic factors concludes that only 15 percent of the rise of income inequality since 1979 can be attributed to them. As she summarizes her findings, "The results of this detailed analysis indicate that changes in family composition and family size account for about 15 percent of the rise in U.S. income inequality, while changes in income account for the remaining rise in inequality. Most of this rise is due to increases in wage inequality."[15] Thus, neither economic causes nor demographic causes can fully explain rising income inequality in the United States.

Institutional Causes

The most convincing explanation for rising income inequality lies in an examination of institutional and political factors.

One is the decline in labor unions. The peak of unionization in the United States was 30 percent in 1960. In 2012, union membership was down to 11 percent.[16] One could note forces in a modern economy pushing union membership downward. For example, rising productivity in manufacturing has led to absolute reductions in the number of production workers even as output increases. Furthermore, employment has shifted out of goods production and distribution industries (manufacturing, wholesale trade, transportation, and warehousing), where unions were traditionally strong, and into service-type industries, such as retail trade and health services, where unions had not been prominent. But those forces are at play in other modern rich nations without a similar effect on unionization. When the U.S. unionization rate was 30 percent in 1960, the rate in Canada was 32 percent. It is still around 30 percent there.[17] Given that both economies are subject to the same market forces, how can we explain the precipitous drop in U.S. unionization while in Canada the rate is where it was forty years ago? Jacob Hacker and Paul Pierson argue that the difference in labor law in the two countries account for union coverage shrinking in the United States and not in Canada. Some Canadian provinces have laws that allow for card check certification and first contract arbitration. Provinces ban the hiring of permanent strike replacements and employer interference into unionization campaigns. In contrast, anti-union action by employers in the United States has met little resistance by government authority. As they point out, inaction as well as action can undercut the power of unions. "The absence of an updating of industrial relations policy has had brutal effects on the long-term prospects of organized labor."[18] A major labor law reform bill promoted by organized labor in 1978 that would have accomplished an updating of labor policies by banning the use of strike replacements was supported by a majority of the House and Senate and President Jimmy Carter, all Democrats. However, it was derailed by a filibuster in the Senate, supported by some Democrats, and was never enacted.[19]

Of course the waning power of labor unions is not the only factor to explain the tremendous rise of income shares at the top of the distribution. Rather, a large part of the explanation lies in the increasing political power and effective organization of business interests, including businesses whose clients are at the top 1 percent of the income distribution, such as mutual funds and other financial firms. As income going to the top end of the distribution has been rising, they raise funding to influence political outcomes in Washington and state capitals by lobbying and political contributions. The failure of progressive labor law legislation is only one example of their success in influencing social policy. More examples follow in the next section.

Political Causes

Economists stress market forces and technology as causes of rising income inequality. Political scientists stress the median voter theorem in their analysis of why income inequality has been rising.[20] But neither of those views takes into account organized interests. In an article called "Winner-Take-All Politics" (2010), which they later developed into a book with the same title, Jacob Hacker and Paul Pierson present a cogent empirical story about the sharp rise of income shares at the top developed around three claims. First, government involvement in the modern economy is broad and deep. Second, policy transformation occurs through both enactment and non-enactment. Third, shifts in organized interests are a major force in policy change.

The first, government involvement in the modern economy is broad and deep, flies against the conventional view among most economists that the distribution of pre-tax income is the result of market forces. The role of government, they argue, is limited to the fiscal side: taxation and transfers that can alter the market distribution of income. This is a naive view. A number of government policies tilt the distribution of pre-tax income in favor of the very top of the income distribution, including:

1. Tort reform and arbitration law trends that curtail power of consumers and stockholders to hold corporation management legally accountable for purported wrongdoing.
2. Special treatment of corporate stock option awards.
3. Restricting access to bankruptcy protection for consumers and business.
4. Extending time of copyright protection for some large firms.
5. Extending time of patent protection for nongeneric drugs.
6. Forbidding Medicare to bargain for lower pharmaceutical prices.

Note that all six of these policies favor corporations and their owners. The current broad and deep involvement of the federal government in the economy is similar to that of the Gilded Age. Long ago, in 1892, John R. Commons, an economics professor at the University of Syracuse, argued that a substantial share of U.S. corporations owed their quasi-monopoly market power to privileges and protections, such as patents and copyrights, bestowed by the federal government.[21] The ensuing storm of protest from business and from economists led to his dismissal by the University of Syracuse. He was right, and he touched a nerve.

The second claim is that policy transformation occurs through both enactment and non-enactment, or what they call "policy drift." Non-enactment occurs through filibusters in the Senate, a tactic increasingly pursued in the polarized body. According to Senate rules, ending a filibuster requires a supermajority of sixty votes. Thus, a determined minority can use the filibuster to block legislation. In the fifty years from 1919 to 1969, fifty-six motions were filed to stop a filibuster, but from 1969 through 2009 there were 1,100 filed, most of them after 1991.[22]

Finally, shifts in organized interests are a major force in policy change. Hacker and Pierson document a huge rise of special-interest organizations in Washington beginning in the 1970s. Corporations with a public affairs office in Washington went from one hundred in 1968 to five hundred by 1978. Further, the three giants of promoting and protecting corporate interests, the National Association of Manufacturers, the Business Roundtable, and the Chamber of Commerce, greatly expanded their membership and budgets after 1970. Needless to say, the headquarters of all three are in Washington, D.C. The National Association of Manufacturers was formerly in New York, but it moved to Washington around 1974.[23]

Labor and consumers, the main countervailing powers to businesses in a capitalist democracy, have no similar weight in Washington. Unions are the only organizations pushing for

Table 3.1. Lobbying Presence
in Washington

Institution	1981	2006
Business	7,059	12,785
Union	369	403
Public interest	237	405

Source: Based on Drutman (2010).

bread-and-butter issues for workers in Washington, yet they have a small fraction of the lobbyists employed by business, and they are falling behind. Other liberal organizations pushing environmental issues, civil rights, and women's issues are also falling behind, as shown in Table 3.1.

An example of the overwhelming numbers of lobbyists representing business interests: there are about one thousand registered Washington lobbyists who list taxes as one of their areas. Yet in the estate tax fight, an issue of great importance for income distribution, only one union lobbyist was available to represent worker and consumer interests.[24]

Although most attention of the media is on election campaign funding, that apparently is not where corporations spend more to influence government outcomes. "Companies generally spend about twelve times more on lobbying than they spend on campaign contributions [political action committees, or PACs]."[25] Lobbying expenditures in Washington, adjusted for inflation, have risen 77 percent since 1998. That is far more than other measures of legislative activity, such as bills introduced (+43 percent), federal budget (+38 percent), and *Federal Register* pages (+18 percent).[26]

Shifts in organized interests favoring the issues of corporations and the wealthy are also reflected in the rise of think tanks funded by conservative interests—to name the most prominent, the American Enterprise Institute (AEI), the Heritage Foundation, the Olin Foundation, the Hoover Institution, and the Cato Institute. They are heavily engaged in lobbying and political suasion on behalf of conservative viewpoints. Older think tanks such as the Brookings Institution and the Twentieth Century Fund (now the Century Fund) could be described as centrist or liberal, and engage in much less advocacy than the new conservative organizations. The Heritage Foundation allocates 20 percent of its budget on public relations and outreach, whereas Brookings allocates 5 percent.[27]

Many if not all of the objectives of business lobbying, election campaigning, and advocacy can be described as rent-seeking. The economic definition of rent-seeking is

> Spending time and money not on the production of real goods and services, but rather on trying to get the government to change the rules so as to make one's business more profitable. This can take various forms, including seeking subsidies on the outputs or the inputs of a business, or persuading the government to change the rules so as to keep out competitors, tolerate or promote collusion between those already engaged in an activity, or make legally compulsory the use of professional services.[28]

In this definition, rent-seeking is the expenditure of resources to make one's slice of the pie—GDP—larger at the expense of someone else's share. Resources so spent are wasted because they do not add to society's total output; they simply change the shares received by each of the parties. Rent-seeking is not always facilitated by government action, as implied by the quoted definition. It can result from government inaction as well as from actions by private parties. Successful rent-seeking that shifts more of national output (income) to the top 1 percent or 0.01 percent may well be the most important cause of rising income inequality at the top of the income distribution over the past forty years in the United States. It is covered here under "political causes" because it is most often facilitated by government action or government failure to act.

In his recent book *The Price of Inequality,* Joseph Stiglitz places rent-seeking front and center in Chapter 2 ("Rent Seeking and the Making of an Unequal Society"). He claims that "some of the most important innovations in business in the last three decades have centered not on making the economy more efficient but on how better to ensure monopoly power or how better to circumvent government regulations intended to align social returns and private rewards."[29] Mankiw argues to the contrary that "there is no good reason to believe that rent seeking by the rich is more pervasive today than it was in the late 1970s."[30] But there is a good reason. The top marginal tax rate was around 70 percent in the late 1970s. It has since been lowered a few times as well as raised and is now 39.6 percent. That means any successful rent-seeking effort by those in the top tax bracket today has an after-tax payoff almost double the size of a similar one in the 1970s.

For example, it is assumed by economists that perfect competition requires parties to transactions to be equally endowed with information. Yet bankers, the sellers of derivatives, have been fighting to keep derivatives in the opaque "over-the-counter" market where the bankers know far more about the derivatives they trade daily than the sometime buyers.

Echoing Commons in 1892, Stiglitz argues that patent law can protect monopoly power. "The details of patent law can extend the life of the patent, reduce entry of new firms, and enhance monopoly power. America's patent laws have been doing exactly that. They are designed not to maximize the pace of innovation but rather to maximize rents."[31]

The failure of government to act in corporate governance provides what might be the largest single cause of rising income inequality at the very top. As is well known, average CEO pay has been growing rapidly since about 1980, with some cyclical ups and downs. But the base of corporate revenues, value added, or stock prices has been growing slower. In other words, CEOs are taking a bigger slice from a moderately growing pie. That is rent-seeking. The losers are lower-level employees and stockholders. But there is not agreement on that issue. In a paper examining why CEO pay has increased so much, the authors develop a model that "can explain the recent rise in CEO pay as an equilibrium outcome of the substantial growth in firm size."[32] Gordon and Dew-Becker are skeptical: "We endorse their idea [principal-agent control of stockholders should be reversed] that managerial power lies behind some of the outsized gains in CEO pay, while also recognizing that stock options created an automatic spillover from the stock market gains of the 1990s directly into executive pay."[33]

It is difficult to show rent-taking with available data. However, Josh Bivins and Lawrence Mishel present evidence showing growth of CEO pay (including options exercised) of the top 350 Standard & Poor (S&P) 500 firms based on sales. By looking at the S&P 500 stock index over many years, they show that when the S&P 500 went up in 1978–2000 (+513 percent), CEO compensation went up much more (+1,279 percent). When the S&P went down in 2000–2012 (−28 percent), CEO compensation went down about the same (−29 percent).[34]

IV

Consumers' Shift to Debt

Recent years have seen a huge rise of household debt, and rising income inequality has likely been a major cause of this increase in debt.[1] Here we will take a look at the rise of debt and examine the econometric evidence that supports the argued link from rising income inequality to the rise of household debt. Debt-to-income ratios rose sharply as growth of household debt far exceeded growth of income. Households' stagnant incomes and rapidly rising house values induced them to take on far more debt, a move facilitated by relaxed credit standards and low interest rates.

Household Debt: National Macro Data

The System of National Accounts financial data indicate that households, combined with nonprofit institutions, were net lenders for most of the long period since the 1960s. That is, their net savings exceeded their net capital formation (primarily residential investment).

Figure 4.1 illustrates that pattern of households shifting from long-term net lenders to net borrowers in relative terms.

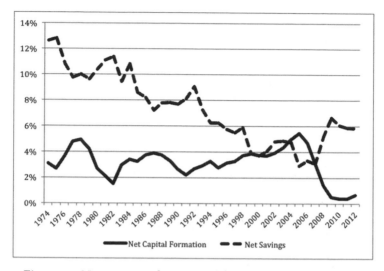

Figure 4.1. Net saving and net capital formation as percentage of disposable income, 1974–2012. *Source:* Bureau of Economic Analysis (n.d.), "National Economic Accounts," Table S.3.a, December 2013.

The top line in the left part of Figure 4.1 is net saving (lending) as a percentage of disposable income. The lower line is net capital formation (primarily residential investment) as a percentage of disposable income. Both are for the household and nonprofit institutions sector. From the mid-1970s to the early 1980s, the share of savings fluctuated around 10 percent of disposable income; thereafter it mostly declined through 2006. The net capital formation (borrowing) share of disposable income fluctuated below 5 percent in the early years, and then in the mid-1990s it began rising to its peak in 2005. By the late 1990s, the net capital formation share moved above the declining net savings share. After 2005, both lines abruptly change direction, so that by 2010 the net savings share is well above the net capital formation share. The fact that households went from a long-term net lending position to a massive net borrowing position beginning in 1999 suggests that the System of National Account data had pointed to an imminent financial crisis.[2]

To get a detailed picture of the rising indebtedness among families alone, excluding nonprofit institutions, requires data from the Survey of Consumer Finances (SCF), which is produced by the Federal Reserve Board every three years. The earliest SCF data is from 1980, and the latest from 2010. Broad variables covered by the SCF are income, assets, and debt of families. Because the SCF collects data on assets that are heavily concentrated among the richest families, in order to be representative and meet validity standards, the sample is designed to capture sufficient numbers of upper-income families.

The dollar value of debt holdings, in real terms, has risen sharply. Table 4.1 presents the median value of debt holdings by debt categories for three years: 1995, 2007, and 2010. (The SCF data are only collected every three years). Note that families with no debt in a given category are excluded from the calculation of the medians. Residential mortgage debt dwarfs the other three categories in size. It includes not just first mortgages on a family's primary residence but also second mortgages, refinancing, home equity loans, and vacation homes. The median family mortgage debt in constant dollars rose from $126,000 in 1995 to $217,000 in 2007. Most of that rise occurred from 2001 to 2004, the period when aggregate mortgage liabilities increased by $2.5 trillion (see Table 4.7). The 1995 to 2007 increase in median real mortgage debt, 73 percent, is many times larger than the increase in median household real income over that period—only 8 percent.[3] It has diminished somewhat since its peak of $225,000 in 2004, reflecting the bursting of the housing price bubble and the resulting reduction of mortgage lending.

Table 4.1. Median Value of Family Debt Holdings (2010 $ thousands)

Year	Primary residence and other residential mortgage debt	Credit card and lines of credit other than residential	Installment loans[a]	Other[b]	Any debt
1995	125.7	6.7	16.4	2.7	29.2
2007	216.9	7.1	13.6	5.2	70.6
2010	207.6	8.6	12.6	4.5	70.7
			Percent change		
1995–2007	72.6%	6.0%	−17.1%	92.6%	141.8%

[a] Includes education, vehicle, and other.
[b] Includes cash value of life insurance loans, pension account loans, margin account loans, and other miscellaneous loans.

Source: Federal Reserve Board (2012).

The largest part of consumer debt is mortgages, as noted above. The Federal Reserve publishes two measures of household debt burden: the Debt Service Ratio (DSR) and the Financial Obligation Ratio (FOR). The DSR measures debt payments as a share of disposable income for all households. The FOR measures mortgage debt, home insurance, property tax, and consumer debt as well as automobile leases as a percentage of disposable income for homeowners only. Both are shown for selected years in Table 4.2. Although both indices are higher in 1995 than in 1980, the individual years' data reveal no trend. In some years before 1995 the indices are higher, and in some years lower. That changes post 1995 when most year-to-year changes are positive. The 2007 values shown are record highs

Table 4.2. Household Debt Burden

First Quarter of Year	DSR	FOR
1980	10.62	15.43
1995	10.90	16.22
2007	12.88	17.70
2014	9.96	15.34

Source: Federal Reserve Board (2014b).

for each index. But following the financial crash and Great Recession, both measures were lower than their 1995 values.

Household Debt by Income Group

Growth in median family residential mortgage debt among different quintiles and deciles of the income distribution over the 1995 to 2007 period was substantial and broadly similar, as reported by the Survey of Consumer Finances and presented in Table 4.3. Shown is the largest debt category, mortgages on primary residences, which increased substantially—from 41 percent in quintile two to 90 percent in the second-from-the-top decile (80.0–89.9).

Based on data from the SCF, Figure 4.2 shows debt-to-income ratios for the top 5 percent of the income distribution and the bottom 95 percent. The authors note about the figure,

> In 1983 the top income group is somewhat more indebted than the bottom group, with a gap of around 20 percentage points. In 2007, the situation was dramatically reversed. The debt-to-income ratio of the bottom group, at 147.3% compared to an initial value of 62.3%, was now more than twice

Table 4.3. Median Family Residential Mortgage Debt by Quintiles, 1995, 2007, and 2010 (2010 $ thousands)

Quintile	1995	2007	2010	Percent change 1995–2007	2007–10
Quintile 1	25.0	41.9	54.6	67.6%	30.3%
Quintile 2	37.9	53.4	65.5	40.9%	22.7%
Quintile 3	50.0	92.9	90.0	85.8%	−3.1%
Quintile 4	77.1	120.5	116.6	56.3%	−3.2%
2nd top decile, 80–89.9	90.6	171.8	158.0	89.6%	−8.0%
Top decile, 90–100	121.7	210.6	241.0	73.0%	14.4%

Source: Federal Reserve Board (2012), Tables 13 95 through 13 07.

as high as that of the top group. Between 1983 and 2007, the debt to income ratio of the bottom group therefore more than doubled while the ratio of the top group remained fluctuating around 60%.[4]

But the figure also shows that the huge run-up of the debt-to-income ratio for the bottom 95 percent occurred in the period after 2001. The authors infer from Figure 4.2 that it is part of the explanation for why consumption inequality has not increased nearly as much as income inequality. That is, the bottom 95 percent of the wealth distribution has taken on much more debt in order to maintain their consumption.

Subprime Mortgages

One of the direct causes of the financial crash was the increased volume of subprime mortgages that were bundled into securities and sold to investors. The collapse of prices for those securitized debt obligations touched off the financial crisis. There

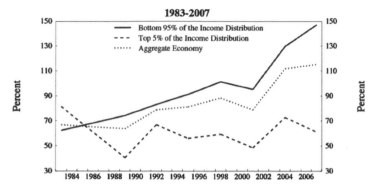

Figure 4.2. Debt-to-income ratios, 1983–2007. *Source:* Reprinted with permission from Michael Kumhof, Romain Ranciere, and Pablo Winant (2013), "Inequality, Leverage and Crises: The Case of Endogenous Default," International Monetary Fund Working Paper, WP/13/249, November, p. 38.

was a stunning rise of subprime mortgage originations from slightly over 400,000 in 1999 to over two million in 2005, the peak year.[5] The total of originations is split between refinancings and purchases. In every year from 1999 through 2006, the refinancing with subprime mortgages is 60 to 75 percent of total originations. A major purpose of mortgage refinancing is to take out cash. As shown in Figure 4.2, the ratio of debt to income for the bottom 95 percent of the wealth distribution shot up sharply, from 90 percent in 2001 to near 150 percent in 2007. Some part of that rise reflects the fivefold increase in subprime mortgages.

That rise has not been geographically concentrated so much as credit score concentrated. In a paper that splits a huge sample of zip codes into quartiles based on credit scores, the bottom quartile is labeled subprime—that is, it has the highest share of households with credit scores of 660 or less. The authors found that the mortgage default rate in 2006 of subprime zip codes was three times higher than the rate in

prime zip codes. Additionally, mortgage credit growth in subprime zip codes (the quartile with the highest share of credit
scores below 660) was two times greater than mortgage credit
growth in prime zip codes (the quartile with the lowest share
of credit scores below 660). Subprime zip codes are not region-
ally concentrated but rather are present in most metropolitan
areas. Correlation between mortgage credit growth and income growth was *negative* in the 2002–05 period, whereas it
was positive in the prior fifteen years. Before the expansion in
subprime mortgage lending, applications for mortgage credit
from subprime zip codes were more likely to be denied than
those from quartiles with higher credit scores. However, from
2002 to 2005, denial rates for subprime zip codes fall dispro-
portionately. An examination of house price indices by zip
code shows that house price gains for subprime zip codes in a
county are greater than gains for non-subprime zip codes.[6]

Christopher Mayer and Karen Pence established that
the use of subprime mortgages is not ubiquitous over states
or metropolitan areas, or in demographic characteristics of
borrowers. Looking at the data by state, they showed that subprime originations as a percentage of all originations in 2005,
the peak year for subprime originations, were 19 percent for the
nation. The four states with the highest concentration of subprime and Alt-A mortgages as reported by the New York Federal Reserve Bank in 2011 had subprime originations in 2005 at
or above the national average: Nevada, 25 percent; Florida, 24
percent; Arizona, 21 percent; and California, 19 percent. The
state shares of subprime originations range from the high of
25 percent in Nevada to the low of 8 percent in West Virginia.
The same data for metropolitan areas in 2005 show much
greater variation. The 2005 average for 107 large metro areas is
20 percent. Memphis and Bakersfield, California, are tied for

first place with 34 percent. Madison, Wisconsin, is in last place with only 9 percent. Anecdotal comparisons that spring to mind in thinking of those three places are that both Memphis and Bakersfield have high shares of minority population, low median incomes, and low levels of educational attainment. Madison is the opposite on all three measures. The top ten places in share of subprime mortgage originations include the most likely suspects because of large house price increases and construction booms: Las Vegas, Miami, and Houston, as well as Detroit, which had well under average price appreciation and certainly no construction boom. Four of the top ten are mid-size California metros far from the coast, some of which had construction booms, and all of which have large Hispanic population shares and low educational attainment.[7]

Mayer and Pence found that subprime lending is not elevated only in metros with strong housing price surges. They cite New York and Boston as places with relatively high house price appreciation, but not much in the way of subprime mortgages. But subprime lending surged in depressed housing markets of the Midwest because conventional lending had diminished. Looking at neighborhoods with zip code data, they found that "subprime mortgages are concentrated in locations with high proportions of black and Hispanic residents, even controlling for the income and credit scores of these zip codes."[8]

Household Debt, Bankruptcies, and House Prices: State Data

The strong rise of household indebtedness documented here was not underpinned by a strong rise of household income. It was underpinned by the housing price bubble and supply-side factors that increased the availability of credit—subprime mortgage lending, low interest rates, relaxed credit standards, and financial deregulation that made residential property more liquid. Both the explosion of debt and fallout from the collapse of the housing price bubble were mostly ubiquitous across states, although four states stand out for larger gains and more severe declines: Arizona, California, Nevada, and Florida. Those are the states that had the highest concentration of toxic real estate assets: subprime and Alt-A mortgages. Although the four states' share of all housing units in the nation is 20 percent, they account for 28 percent of all subprime mortgages and 45 percent of all Alt-A mortgages.[9] The top panel of Table 4.4 summarizes debt, mortgage debt, house prices, and median household income for all states and the District of Columbia from 1999 to 2007 and then to 2012. The bottom panel repeats those measures for the four more volatile states named above. For all states in the period 1999–2007, per capita total debt, mortgage debt, and the house price index rose strongly, while median household income hardly changed, gaining less than 1 percent. But then in the following years, 2007–12, they all moved in the opposite direction, including median household income, which fell almost 6 percent. Large as those swings are, they are more extreme in the four states with high concentrations of subprime and Alt-A mortgages. Note that the data in Table 4.4 are simple averages for states. Excluding the four states from the calculations for the top panel, the picture does not change much. That is, debt and house prices rise somewhat less from 1999 to 2007, and decline somewhat less from 2007 to 2012. The point is that the huge run-up in debt and the housing price bubble cannot be attributed only to toxic mortgages in the four states with high concentrations of such loans.

The sluggish growth of household income by state compared with soaring per capita household debt and house prices

Table 4.4. Household Debt Compared with House Prices and Median Income, 1999–2012

Year	Total debt per capita (2008 $ thousands)	Mortgage debt per capita (2008 $ thousands)	House price index (1991 Q1 = 100)	Median household income (2008 $ thousands)
	Simple averages for 50 states and District of Columbia			
1999	28.7	19.4	138.4	52.7
2007	48.6	35.5	228.5	53.0
2011	46.3	34.2	197.3	48.3
2012	44.3	33.2	189.5	48.2
	Simple average for four states[a]			
1999	34.8	25.9	126.9	51.7
2007	73.1	57.2	257.4	53.3
2011	55.8	42.1	169.0	48.1
2012	51.1	39.3	159.8	45.1

[a] Arizona, California, Florida, and Nevada.

Source: Household debt per capita from Federal Reserve Bank of New York (2013). Median household income in 2010 dollars from U.S. Census Bureau (n.d.), "Current Population Survey." House price index from Federal Housing Finance Agency (2014).

from 1999 to 2007, presented in Table 4.4, points to a precarious financial condition for many households. A surge of personal bankruptcies post 2000 prompted a strong pro-creditor reaction by Congress so that upward trends were abruptly halted in 2006. The Bankruptcy Abuse Prevention and Consumer Protection Act enacted in April 2005 and effective in October of that year briefly slowed the rise. The purpose of the law was to curb the rise of bankruptcies, both business and non-business, by raising the barriers to filings. The declines from 2005 to 2006 are around 75 percent. However, the earlier upward surge was resumed in 2007, so that by 2010 per capita bankruptcies were well above their 1999 levels.[10] The intention of Congress was apparently overtaken by overwhelming financial hardship post 2006. The act of Congress was inspired more by the perception of bankruptcy abuse than by a desire for consumer protection. The characterization of personal bankrupts as deadbeats was probably important for passage of the bill. But that characterization was false. A careful study of non-business bankruptcies found that "Bankrupts' incomes are low at the time of filing, the consequence of about two-thirds of the families reporting a job loss, failure of a small business, a cutback in hours worked, or some other income interruption. But when they are measured by the enduring criteria of education, occupation, and home ownership, about 90% of the debtors qualify as solidly within the middle class."[11]

REGRESSION RESULTS LINKING RISING HOUSEHOLD
DEBT TO RISING INCOME INEQUALITY: STATE DATA

A central argument of this book is that the huge run-up in household debt that was one of the major causes of the financial crisis, and the Great Recession was itself in part a manifestation of the long rise of income inequality. That possible link of rising income inequality to rising household debt has been explored econometrically using the New York Federal Reserve Bank data on household debt by state, 1999 to 2010. The key advantage of that data is that it provides time-series data on household debt for all states, enabling the estimation of panel data regression equations. Panel data equations are less fraught with the estimation problems of time-series data, and they have much larger sample sizes. Instead of having a sample limited to the number of years, a panel regression sample size is equal to the number of time periods, twelve years in this case, multiplied by the number of entities, fifty states and the District of Columbia, or 612. Panel regression equations have been estimated to measure the connection, if any, between rising income inequality and rising household debt. The details about those estimated equations are presented in an appendix to this chapter. Here the substantive results are presented in a non-technical manner.

Table 4.5 shows the estimated elasticities from the panel regression equations presented and explained in the appendix. These elasticities are the percent change in per capita household debt with respect to a 1 percent change in the variable named, holding all else equal. The key variable is the income share of the bottom 80 percent by state and year, the first elasticity shown. Its estimated value is −0.2. That means that a 1 percent *fall* of the state income share (rising income inequality) for the bottom 80 percent of households is expected to produce a *rise* of 0.2 percent in state per capita household debt three years later, other things being equal. In other words, rising inequality is accompanied by rising household debt with a lag of three years. The estimated elasticity is highly significant, as noted in the table.

The other elasticities have the expected signs—negative for the national unemployment rate and positive for the state house price index and state median household income. All are highly significant except for the state median household income variable. Note that the largest effect on per capita household debt is the state house price index, with an elasticity of +0.3. The interpretation of that result is that rising house prices induced a perception of enhanced wealth, which motivated households to borrow more.

Table 4.5. Elasticities of Per Capita Household Debt with Respect to Income Inequality and Other Measures by State and Year

Variable	Elasticity
State income share bottom 80%, lagged three years	-0.2^{b}
U.S. unemployment rate	-0.1^{a}
State house price index	$+0.3^{a}$
State median household income	$+0.1^{c}$

[a] significant at .001 level
[b] significant at .01 level
[c] significant at .05 level

Source: Author's calculations.

These results, elaborated in the appendix, of course do not prove a causal link from a diminishing state share of income received by the four lower income quintiles (rising income inequality) to rising household debt, but they do support the argument of a causal link. If the equations showed a positive effect or no significant effect of rising income inequality on debt, then there would be little inducement to further work supporting that claim. But these results beg for stronger support or refutation.

Stronger support is provided in an article by Robert Hockett and Daniel Dillon. Their careful econometric analysis shows that a rise of the very top income share, the share of the 0.1 percent, is followed two years later by a rise in all household debt per capita, ceteris paribus. The same holds true on the downside. A decline of the income share of the top 0.1 percent is associated with a drop in household debt two years later. The authors argue: "This positive feedback loop presents evidence of the hypothesized relationship between inequality and debt, namely that as the wealthy amass more of the aggregate income, the average household ramps up its borrowing to maintain accustomed living standards."[12]

In another paper that covers some of the same material on inequality and household debt as this book, the authors estimate time-series regression equations relating measures of debt to measures of inequality and other variables. Estimated coefficients on their inequality variables are not statistically significant in about half of the cases. That may reflect a flaw in the choice of some inequality variables—namely, the labor share of national income. As noted in Chapter II, the top 1 percent's share of labor income has doubled since 1969. Thus, labor share does not fully capture the rise of inequality (see Table 2.2). Also, the authors use quarterly data with a sample size of only 93, whereas the sample size here is 407.[13]

REGRESSION RESULTS LINKING RISING
HOUSEHOLD DEBT TO RISING INCOME INEQUALITY:
NATIONAL DATA

This second use of regression to estimate association between income inequality and household debt shifts from a state to a national focus using the Consumer Expenditure Survey (CEX) data by income quintiles for the years 1984 through 2007. The interview survey data from the CEX of the Bureau of Labor Statistics (BLS) is the only annual survey that provides after-tax income by income class as well as change in liabilities by income class. The observations in that analysis are average dollar amounts by quintile and year, not individual consumer units.

In addition to covering numerous out-of-pocket consumer expenditure categories, the CEX also collects before and after-tax income data, household characteristics, as well as some financial data. The consumer units are subdivided into five income quintiles. For most of the years of the continuous annual survey, 1984–2003, the quintile data excluded consumer units that did not report their income. The numbers of such consumer units were shown in the annual reports. They amounted to about 16 percent of all consumer units. Beginning in 2004, the BLS imputed incomes for non-reporting households, and so the distribution by quintile included all consumer units. Before then, CEX reported average income was well below the average income reported on the Census Bureau's Current Population Survey (CPS). The effect of imputation was to raise substantially the ratio of CEX pre-tax income to CPS pre-tax income, making the two series closer. In 2003, before income imputation, CEX income was 75 percent of CPS income. In 2004, after income imputation, that ratio rose to 91 percent.[14] CEX data for previous years were not revised, and so the CEX for 2004 forward is not quite comparable to earlier years.

As with the state regression analysis, the dependent variable is a measure of household debt by years and by income quintile. The national panel regression equation by quintile and year, presented in the appendix, uses the Theil index of inequality (a rise means increased income inequality). That is the variable of central interest.

Economic Insecurity

All of the evidence presented in this chapter on the increasing amounts of debt taken on by households suggests that they might have been feeling more anxious about their economic situation than in the past. There is a statistical series that attempts to capture not the feeling of anxiety but rather the objective fact of financial insecurity. The 2010 Economic Security Index (ESI) is designed to capture that. The measure is based on panel data and at present covers most of the years from 1986 through 2010. The major data source used in constructing the index is the Survey of Income and Program Participation (SIPP) of the Census Bureau. Also used are the BLS Consumer Expenditure Survey and the University of Michigan's Panel Study of Income Dynamics.

> The ESI is designed to fill a gap in existing theoretical and empirical analyses of economic security grounded in panel data on economic status. Prior research has focused primarily on individual sources of insecurity, such as earnings volatility and the incidence of large medical expenditures. The ESI by contrast represents the first attempt to incorporate several key influences—income declines, medical spending shocks, and financial wealth buffers—into a single unified measure.[15]

For each household i in the large sample, a dichotomous variable r_i is calculated. If the year-to-year loss of discretionary income is 25 percent or more, $r_i = 1$. Discretionary income is total household income less out-of-pocket medical expenses and debt service. Sufficient liquid assets for a household can offset some or all the decline in discretionary income. The ESI in any year is the weighted sum of the r scores over the sample size.

Figure 4.3 presents the ESI for selected years (a high ESI indicates greater economic insecurity) for all households. Al-

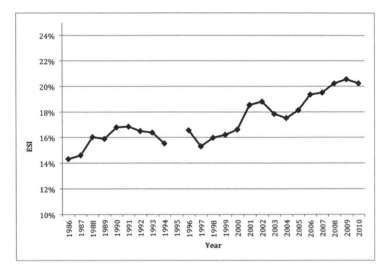

Figure 4.3. Economic Security Index (ESI), all households, 1986–
2010. *Source:* Hacker (2015).

though there are ups and downs associated with cyclical influences, the ESI has a decidedly upward trend, rising from
around 14 percent in 1986 to over 20 percent in the most recent years, 2008–10.

    The ESI has been calculated for individual income quin-
tiles as well as all households. The quintile data are not published, but they were provided by one of the authors, and these
data are presented in Table 4.6.[16] The ESI tends to be smaller
for higher income quintiles, except that the fifth quintile is
above (higher economic insecurity) the fourth in some years.
It appears that the ESI captures something not reflected in the
common objective measures of hardship: the unemployment
and poverty rates. Note that although unemployment and
poverty were lower in 2004 than in 1991, the ESI was much
higher in 2004 for the middle three quintiles.

Table 4.6. Economic Security Index, All Households and Quintiles, Selected Years

	1991	2004	2009
All households	16.90%	17.50%	20.50%
Quintile 1	26.30%	20.80%	29.50%
Quintile 2	17.60%	21.20%	22.60%
Quintile 3	14.30%	17.30%	18.90%
Quintile 4	12.50%	15.40%	16.20%
Quintile 5	13.50%	12.90%	15.50%
Unemployment rate	6.80%	5.50%	9.30%
Poverty rate	14.20%	12.70%	14.30%

Source: Author's compilation of ESI by quintile from Hacker (2015). Unemployment rate from Council of Economic Advisers (2013). Poverty rate from DeNavas-Walt, Proctor, and Smith (2011).

Why Household Debt Soared

The argument that the rise of consumer indebtedness is linked to income inequality is well stated by Stiglitz.

> The negative impact of stagnant real incomes and rising income inequality on aggregate demand was largely offset by financial innovation in risk management and lax monetary policy that increased the ability of households to finance consumption by borrowing, especially in the United States. . . . But increasing household indebtedness was not sustainable. Or rather what was perceived to be sustainable was dependent on artificially inflated asset prices that created the illusion that household wealth was increasing at a faster pace than their debt. The support for the bubble thus depended on

expansionary monetary policy together with financial sector innovation leading to ever-increasing
asset prices that allowed households virtually un-
limited access to credit.[17]

Christopher Carroll, Misuzu Otsuka, and Jiri Slacalek argue
that the use of enhanced housing values to support consumption is a long-standing pattern, and they find a substantial effect that may or may not be as large as the effect of enhanced
financial wealth. They do not consider any role for rising income inequality. Other writers point to extreme leveraging by
consumers as contributing to the financial crash but ascribe
no role to stagnant incomes and increasing income inequality. Their listed causes for that leveraging are all on the supply
side: financial innovation, rising house prices, subprime mortgage securitization, low interest rates, and massive inflows of
foreign credit.[18]

The absolute and relative rise in household debt documented in this chapter was facilitated by a number of factors. One was the advent of subprime and Alt-A mortgages
aggressively pushed by mortgage lenders who understood that
investment banks were eager to buy them and bundle them into
bonds—securitized debt obligations. Another was the development of mortgage refinancing, home equity loans, and home equity lines of credit, financial instruments not widely available to
households until the 1990s. "Two pieces of legislation, the Monetary Control Act of 1980 and the Garn-St Germain Act of 1982,
unlocked this wealth [residential property worth 106 percent
of GDP]. The new laws made it easier for households to refinance their mortgages and borrow against the value of their
homes." Also, Congress was pushing government-sponsored
Fannie Mae and Freddie Mac to boost mortgage lending to

underserved households.[19] Finally, unusually low interest rates following the onset of recession in 2000–2001 and after the World Trade Center attack in 2001 were continued until 2005. As Stiglitz noted about that period leading up to the financial crash and Great Recession, "Greenspan lowered interest rates flooding the market with liquidity. With so much excess capacity in the economy, not surprisingly, the lower interest rates did not lead to more investment in plant and equipment. They worked—but only by replacing the tech bubble with a housing bubble, which supported a consumption and real estate boom."[20] All of those supply-side factors raised the availability of credit. But increased supply does not ensure increased demand for credit by households. The rise of demand was for two purposes: to buy homes and to take out cash for maintaining consumption.

Borrowing to buy an asset with an expected growth in value well above the cost of borrowing is not irrational. As the data above show, most of their borrowing and most of their outstanding debt has been for residential property, the dominant part (60 percent in 2007) of their non-financial assets. Consumers knew house prices were rising rapidly from 1995 to 2006 while mortgage interest rates were trending down. The rate of house price appreciation, 10 percent per year during 1997–2006, was well above the average interest rate on a conventional mortgage for that period, 6.8 percent.[21] Thus it was wealth enhancing to borrow to buy a house as long as house prices continued to rise.

The ten-year rapid rise of house prices lured consumers into thinking that the future would be similar to the past. A Case-Shiller survey of home buyers in the spring of 2005 revealed that the median expectation of house price appreciation for the next ten years was 7 percent annually. In fact, house prices nationally declined 25 percent from the spring of 2005, when the Case-Shiller survey was taken, to the spring of 2009.[22]

Not all the debt that shows up as mortgage debt, by far the largest debt category for households (see Table 4.1), represents borrowing to purchase a home. Many households tapped that increased wealth with second or junior mortgages, cash-out refinancing, and home equity loans or lines of credit. Indeed, an analysis by two authors of what existing homeowners did in reaction to their increased home values argues that rising home values lured consumers into taking on more debt. The effect they calculate is large. They find "an elasticity of borrowing with respect to increased home equity of 0.60. Alternatively we find that households borrow 25 to 30 cents on each additional dollar of home equity from 2002 to 2006."[23] Recall that, as mentioned above, rising house prices have the largest positive impact on per capita state debt.

Table 4.7 shows that the rise in such cash extraction from residential property accounted for about one-half of the spectacular rise in mortgage debt from 2004 to 2007. But with the bursting of the housing price bubble in 2005–06, those credit sources were shut down for most households. The burden of mortgage debt as a percentage of the market value of households' real estate jumped from just over 40 percent in 2004 to 50 percent in 2007 and 60 percent in 2010. In 2007 home equity loans outstanding were $1.1 trillion, compared with $0.4 trillion in 2000. Note that the changes in mortgage liabilities and cash-out from mortgages became large negative amounts in 2010. That sharp turnaround does not simply reflect foreclosures and write-offs of household liabilities by financial institutions after the financial crash in 2008. A Federal Reserve

Table 4.7. Change in Mortgage Liabilities and Change in Cash-Out from Mortgaged Properties, 1992–2010

Year	Change in residential mortgage liabilities ($ billions)	Change in cash-out from residential mortgages ($ billions)	Change in cash-out as % of change in mortgages	Residential mortgage liabilities as % of market value
1992	580	130	22.3%	39.1%
1995	479	236	49.4%	41.2%
1998	735	478	65.0%	41.8%
2001	1,267	324	25.5%	39.2%
2004	2,535	1,286	50.7%	41.5%
2007	2,711	1,351	49.8%	50.7%
2010	−616	−1,077	174.8%	60.0%

Source: Change in residential mortgage liabilities, three-year intervals, calculated from Federal Reserve Board (2014a), Table L.100; cash-out calculated from applying SCF percent shares, Table 14, to aggregate mortgage liabilities. Liabilities as a percent of market value calculated from Federal Reserve Board (2014a), Tables B.100 and L.100.

Board analysis shows that households have voluntarily paid down their debt.[24]

What did households do with all that borrowed money? The shifting relative distribution of households' consumption provides some insight into what they have been spending on, as shown in Table 4.8. That table shows relative expenditure shares for selected categories of consumption for all households and by income quintile, 1984 to 2007. The first column presents the relative shares for all households for selected years. The first category includes food, apparel, and transportation. It fell almost seven percentage points for all households from 1984 to 2007. Each quintile showed similar declines. The three

Table 4.8. Expenditure Shares by Selected Categories and Quintile, 1984 and 2007

	All	Quintile 1	Quintile 2	Quintile 3	Quintile 4	Quintile 5
1984						
Food, apparel, and transportation	40.6%	39.6%	42.6%	42.7%	41.1%	38.8%
Shelter	15.5%	18.9%	15.8%	15.5%	14.8%	15.0%
Health care	4.8%	5.9%	6.8%	5.7%	4.3%	3.5%
Education	1.4%	3.1%	1.1%	1.0%	1.0%	1.3%
Sum of three	21.7%	27.9%	23.7%	22.2%	20.1%	19.8%
2007						
Food, apparel, and transportation	33.8%	34.4%	35.4%	36.0%	35.6%	31.1%
Shelter	20.2%	24.2%	21.5%	19.9%	19.5%	19.5%
Health care	5.7%	7.2%	7.9%	6.7%	5.7%	4.4%
Education	1.9%	3.0%	1.1%	1.3%	1.2%	2.6%
Sum of three	27.8%	34.4%	30.5%	27.9%	26.4%	26.5%

Source: Bureau of Labor Statistics (n.d.), "Consumer Expenditure Survey, 1984–2010."

categories that have had increased relative shares—shelter, health care, and education—are shown separately. Shelter includes the major costs of owning (mortgage interest, property taxes, insurance, and maintenance) as well as renting. Not included are utilities, appliances, and furniture. Health care includes only out-of-pocket spending, not expenses covered by private insurance, Medicare, or Medicaid.

Note that in the first year, 1984, the share spent on food, apparel, and transportation, 40.6 percent, was almost two times greater than the share spent on the three other categories, 21.7 percent. But gradually the share spent on food, apparel, and transportation dropped, while the share spent on shelter, health care, and education rose. That same pattern of increased shares for shelter and health care is repeated in all five quintiles. The share spent on shelter, the largest of the three, was over 15 percent for all households in 1984. By 2007 the share spent on shelter by all households was above 20 percent, ranging from a high of 24 percent in the first quintile to about 20 percent in the other four quintiles. The share spent on education in the first two quintiles did not increase from 1984 to 2007, but it doubled in the highest income quintile.

Aside from the much-noted increased demand for shelter, health care, and education over the past decades, their prices have risen much faster than inflation, while the prices for food, apparel, and transportation have risen at or below inflation. Table 4.9 presents the percentage growth of the Consumer Price Index (CPI) for those categories as well as all items from 1982–84 to 2007. The all items index rose 107 percent, a doubling of the cost of living in about twenty-five years. The shelter index rose more—140 percent—and the health care index jumped over 250 percent. Largest of all are the increases in the major components of the education price index—

**Table 4.9. Percentage Rise of Consumer Price Index, All
Items and Selected Categories, 1982–84 to 2007**

Category	Percentage change, 1982–84 to 2007
All items	107.3%
Food and beverages	103.3%
Apparel	19.0%
Transportation	84.7%
Shelter	140.6%
Medical care	251.1%
Education[a]	
Tuition, school fees, and childcare	394.1%
Education books and supplies	320.4%

[a] Education CPI now published on a December 1997 base = 100, and so it is not comparable with these percent changes.

Source: Bureau of Labor Statistics (n.d.), "Consumer Price Index," 2013.

tuition, fees, and child care, up almost 400 percent, and books and supplies, up 320 percent.

Why did the prices for shelter, education, and medical care rise so much more than the overall price level? One reason is that they are not in competition with cheap imports, unlike electronics and apparel. But the more salient reason for this analysis is that the demand of the top 10 percent for those categories must have expanded strongly with their expanded share of income. Income elasticity of demand for them most certainly is plus one or higher. In Figure 4.4 the trends in those CPI components are compared with the trend of income share for the top 10 percent, 1993 through 2012 or 2013. During that period the income share of the top 10 percent rose from just under 40 percent to just over 48 percent. That gain must have

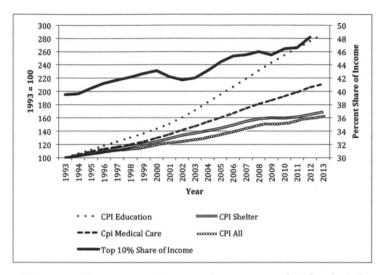

Figure 4.4. Top 10 percent income share compared with selected CPI categories, 1993–2013. *Sources:* Top 10 percent income share from Alvaredo et al. (n.d.). CPI from Bureau of Labor Statistics (n.d.), "Consumer Price Index."

strongly boosted demand for shelter, education, and medical care among the top 10 percent, thus putting upward pressure on prices for those items. Figure 4.4 illustrates how similar the income share trend is to the price trends. Of course that does not prove that rising income inequality at the top pulled up those prices, but the visual correlation is suggestive of such an effect.

Those categories—shelter, health care, and education— are taking a much bigger bite out of households' spending than in the past, and they are not expenditures that can be postponed, such as replacing the car or taking a vacation trip. The immediacy of such demands, combined with decades of stagnant household incomes for most, must have made the

easy availability of credit to be an almost irresistible solution
to the problem of households' squeezed budgets. This analysis of what happened to households' relative consumption is
another support for the argument that stagnant incomes and
rising income inequality led to an explosion of debt.

Atif Mian and Amir Sufi note, "We find little evidence
that borrowing in response to increased house prices is used
to purchase new homes or investment properties. We also
find no evidence that home equity-based borrowing is used
to pay down credit card balances. . . . We find that a total of
$1.45 trillion of the rise in household debt from 2002 to 2006
is attributable to existing homeowners borrowing against the
increased value of their homes. That translates to 2.8% of GDP
per year."[25]

The data presented in this chapter show that the money
taken out from appreciating housing was *not* used to pay
down debt because indebtedness rose. Rather it was used to
support consumption in the face of stagnant income. "Money
extracted from increased home equity is *not* used to purchase
new real estate or pay down high credit card balances, which
suggests that borrowed funds may be used for real outlays (i.e.,
consumption or home improvement)."[26] That point has been
made by others as well. "Where did the borrowings go? Some
have asserted that it went to investments in stocks. However, if
this were the case, then stocks as a share of total assets would
have increased over this period, which it did not (it fell from 13
to 7 percent between 2001 and 2007). . . . Instead middle class
households experiencing stagnating incomes, expanded their
debt almost exclusively in order to finance consumption expenditures."[27] Edward Wolff asks if debt was increased in order
to support normal consumption or to expand consumption.
Analyzing the Consumer Expenditure Survey data over that

period, Wolff concludes, "Thus the CEX data, like the NIPA data, show no acceleration in consumer spending during the debt splurge of the 2000s. As a result it can be concluded that the debt build-up of the 2000s went for normal consumption, not enhanced consumption."[28]

This chapter on consumers' debt and Chapter II on income distribution lay out the facts of stagnant incomes and rising income inequality and the unusually large increase of consumer debt beginning in the mid-1990s that culminated in the financial crash and the Great Recession. Econometric evidence presented in this chapter links rising income inequality to the expansion of household debt, an expansion that was unsustainable. If the Great Recession was in part caused by the big rise in household debt, and that rise in debt was in part the result of stagnant incomes and increased income inequality for three decades, then surely increasing income inequality matters. It matters for understanding how to prevent another big recession. It matters for understanding why the economic recovery has been so sluggish. What is required is a theory to link long-term rising income inequality to a huge rise of unsustainable household debt. The next chapter, on consumption theory, addresses that issue.

Appendix
PANEL REGRESSION ANALYSIS OF STATE DATA

The left-hand or dependent variable in every estimated equation is a measure of per capita household debt by state and year. The key right-hand variable in every equation is the share of aggregate income of quintiles one through four by state and year. The central importance for this study of the estimated panel regression equations is that they support the hypothesis of a positive link between rising income inequality and rising household debt.

Descriptive statistics, means and standard deviations, for all of the variables used are shown in Table 4.10 for three years: 1999, 2007, and 2010. The choice of years is not arbitrary. The first year of the household debt series by state is 1999. The last year before the financial crisis and Great Recession is 2007, and 2010 is the last available year. Most of the variables presented are covered for the same period in Table 4.4. One new variable is the income share of quintiles one through four. Another new variable is the U.S. unemployment rate. That is a national variable that does not vary by state, and hence its standard deviation for each year shown is zero. Note that the income share shows a slight decline of 0.9 of a percentage point from 1999 to 2010—in other words rising income inequality. But in the previous eleven-year period, 1988–99, that share of income to the bottom four quintiles dropped more than three percentage points. Nonetheless, the moderate drop of income share (rising inequality) since 1999 appears to have a positive effect on per capita debt.

Three debt panel regression equations are estimated. The left-hand variables are total debt, mortgage debt, and other debt per capita by state and year. One of the assumptions of regression using time-series data is that the left-hand variable Y_t is stationary. That is, it does not have a stochastic trend. That assumption is rarely satisfied with economic data. The common way to avoid that problem is to express Y_t in first differences—that is, $(Y_t - Y_{t-1})$. There may be important determinants of the Y variables that are not included among the right-hand variables. Such omissions result in biased estimates of regression coefficients. In the case of panel regression, the most common omitted variables are place fixed effects that vary by entity (states in this case) but not by time. The solution

Table 4.10. Descriptive Statistics, 1999, 2007, and 2010

Variables	1999		2007		2010	
	Mean	SD	Mean	SD	Mean	SD
Real total household debt per capita (2008 $ thousands)	28.7	7.4	48.6	15.3	44.7	13.0
Real household mortgage debt per capita (2008 $ thousands)	19.4	7.1	35.5	15.8	32.7	11.6
Real household other debt per capita (2008 $ thousands)	9.3	0.9	13.1	1.7	12.0	1.6
Real household median income (2008 $ thousands)	52.7	7.6	53.0	7.7	50.1	7.5
House price index (1991 Q1 = 100)	138.4	21.0	228.5	42.6	200.9	37.8
Income shares quintiles 1 through 4	51.9	2.5	51.5	2.6	51.0	2.4
U.S. unemployment rate	4.2	0.0	4.6	0.0	9.6	0.0

Source: Household debt per capita from Federal Reserve Bank of New York (2011). Author's compilation of bankruptcy filings from U.S. Courts (n.d.). Median household income in 2010 dollars from DeNavas-Walt, Proctor, and Smith (2011). House price index from Federal Housing Finance Agency (2014). Unemployment rate from Council of Economic Advisers (2013).

for such omitted variables is to express the included variables as first differences over time because then possibly omitted variables that do not vary over time would drop out. That may deal with the problem of non-stationary variables, but one cannot be sure. The panel regression equations are estimated in log differences, which is equivalent to percent changes.

There may be time fixed effects that vary over time but

are constant across states in any year. One solution for that problem is to include a variable that varies by year but is constant across states in any one year. The U.S. unemployment rate variable presumably deals with the problem of time fixed effects and so is included in all three debt equations.

The panel regression equations for estimating changes in household debt are shown in Table 4.11. All three equations are estimated as fixed effects with robust standard errors. All variables are in log difference form. That presumably eliminates state fixed effects that do not vary by time. The share of income for the first through fourth income quintiles by state and year is the key right-hand variable. A plausible assumption is that changes in debt respond with a lag to changes of income distribution among the bottom 80 percent of households. Having no theory as to how long such a lag may be, trial and error estimation with no lag up to a four-year lag revealed a three-year lag as consistently negative and significant. In each of the three debt equations, the coefficient on the income share variable is negative, as expected (a fall in income share is associated with a rise in per capita debt), and significant.

The other three right-hand variables in the debt equations are likely determinants of household debt: unemployment, house prices, and median household income. The unemployment rate is negative as expected (higher unemployment lowers debt) and significant. Both the house price index and median household income variables have positive coefficients and are statistically significant, with the exception that the median income coefficient in the equation for other debt is not significant.

These results tentatively support the argument that rising income inequality results in rising household debt, and the estimated effect is not trivial. The equations in Table 4.11 are estimated in first differences of logs, and so the coefficients

**Table 4.11. Estimated Panel Regression Equations, Log Difference
in Household Debt Per Capita by Year (1999–2010) and State**

Right-hand variables (all are log differences)	Left-hand variables (all are log differences)		
	Total household debt per capita	Household mortgage debt per capita	Other household debt per capita
	Coefficients and *t*-statistics (robust standard errors)		
State income share, quintiles	−0.186	−0.229	−0.118
1–4 lagged three years	(−2.7)	(−2.6)	(−2.0)
U.S. unemployment rate	−0.083	−0.095	−0.055
	(−8.1)	(−8.0)	(−0.4)
State house price index	+0.350	+0.383	+0.269
	(+9.9)	(+9.4)	(+8.5)
State median household income	+0.106	+0.133	+0.050
	(+2.1)	(+2.0)	(+1.0)
Constant	+0.035	+0.047	+0.010
	(+27.0)	(+32.0)	(+9.6)
n	407	407	407
R^2 within	0.38	0.32	0.34
R^2 between	0.26	0.41	0.04
R^2 overall	0.37	0.32	0.32

Source: Author's calculations.

indicate percent changes of the left-hand variables, the per
capita debt measures, resulting from a 1 percent change in a
particular right-hand variable. The coefficients are estimated
elasticities. Thus their values can be compared. However, the
differences between coefficients of any variable are not statisti-

cally significant, and so one cannot infer, for example, that the change of income shares has a larger effect on mortgage debt than on all debt or on other debt. In every equation the largest coefficient is on the state house price index, indicating that a 1 percent rise in house prices is associated with anywhere from a 0.4 percent rise in per capita mortgage debt (equation 2) to a 0.3 percent rise in other debt (equation 3), ceteris paribus. That suggests that the rise of house prices was important for the increase of household debt. Note that the coefficients on the per capita income variable are much smaller, ranging from +0.05 to 0.13, indicating that a 1 percent rise of per capita income is associated with a rise in debt of only about 0.1 percent.

This result linking rising income inequality to rising household debt is illustrative and not definitive for a number of reasons. First, the inferred one-way causality—rising house prices leading to rising debt—could be two-way; that is, rising debt may contribute to rising house prices. Second, using average state data, there is a risk of an ecological fallacy—namely, drawing inferences about individual household behavior from averages for all households in a state. For example, the households in a state going into debt may be different from the households losing ground in the income distribution. With these caveats in mind, the claim that these results support the causal hypothesis that rising income inequality leads to rising household debt is tentative and begs for future thorough econometric investigation.

The most novel feature of the estimation procedure used is to let one variable, the national unemployment rate, stand for the time fixed effect. That is, it varies by year but not by state. The conventional way to deal with time fixed effects in panel regression is to introduce dummy variables, one less than the number of time periods. The equations were estimated again, dropping the national unemployment rate and adding ten dummy variables because the time period is eleven years. Rather than show those alternative estimated panel regressions (they are available upon request), the results are summarized here. First, the key right-hand variable, the share of state income in quintiles one through four, is always negative as expected but is never significant. Second, the time dummy variables as a group are highly significant in all three equations, with F statistics ranging from 53 to 254. Third, the overall R^2 values are much higher, ranging from 0.79 to 0.65. One could argue that the conventional way to deal with time fixed effects is more appropriate than the use of a single national variable. Nonetheless, the key right-hand variable measuring income share of the bottom four quintiles is negative as expected in both sets of equations.

The equations shown in Table 4.11 were estimated yet again with a shorter time frame: 1999–2007, eliminating the years of the financial crash and onset of the Great Recession—the reason being that the effect of rising income inequality on the change in debt would be much less or absent with those shocks that shut down access to credit. But the time frame of the panel, eleven years, was already questionably short. Not surprisingly, those estimated alternative equations are poor, with two of the four right-hand variables insignificant in each equation. Even so, the key right-hand variable, the income share of the bottom four quintiles, is negative as expected, but not significant.

PANEL REGRESSION ANALYSIS OF NATIONAL DATA

A panel regression equation is estimated relating consumer liabilities to income, an income inequality measure, and two other right-hand variables. The equation is estimated with fixed effects over twenty-four years and five quintiles. For all the reasons noted above about estimation of the state panel regressions, the equation is estimated in first differences. Also, there is a time fixed effect variable—that is, it varies by year but not by quintile. It is the Theil index of income inequality.

The dependent or left-hand variable in the equation is net change in average annual liabilities in each quintile (1–5 quintiles) and each year (1984–2007). Net change in average annual liabilities is defined by the CEX as the sum of change in mortgage principal (primary residence as well as vacation home, other properties, and home equity loans and home equity lines of credit), change in principal balance on vehicle loans, and change in amount owed to other creditors, primarily credit card balances. The first independent or right-hand variable is change in average annual after-tax income in a quintile and a year. The inequality variable, the Theil index, varies by year and not by quintile, and so it is a time fixed effect in the equation.

The Theil index of income inequality is as reported in the CPS. A rising Theil index indicates increasing income inequality. The expectation is that there is a positive relationship between the change in the Theil index and the change in average household liabilities. That is, with rising income inequality, measured by a positive change in the Theil index, households increase their liabilities to maintain their consumption, as argued by some of the authors cited and as inferred from the state panel regression analysis. Access to credit can cushion the effect of increased income inequality upon consumption.

The CEX data are subject to an important break beginning in 2004 when income of non-reporting households (formerly 16 percent or so of the CEX sample) is imputed as explained above. The 1984–2003 data are not comparable with the 2004–07 data. Rather than end the estimation period in

Table 4.12. Estimated Panel Regression Equation. Change in Household Liabilities by Year (1984–2007) and Quintile

Right-hand variables	Coefficients and t-statistics
Constant	7,476
	(11.7)
Change in after-tax income, lagged	0.977
	(2.1)
Year dummy	1,931
	(1.3)
Interaction term (Year dummy × income)	0.127
	(3.4)
Change in Theil index	42,277
	(1.6)
R^2	
Within	0.41
Between	0.99
Overall	0.42
n	110

Source: Author's calculations.

2003, a dummy variable is introduced equal to one in the years of income imputation, 2004–07, and zero in the prior years. The dummy variable is interacted with the average after-tax income by quintile and year. Of course both the dummy and the interaction term must be expressed as levels, not changes. As changes they would both equal zero. Although the CEX data are available through 2010, the estimation period for the equation is limited to 1984–2007 in order to exclude the recession and financial crisis years. The liabilities and income data are from the CEX. All dollar amounts are expressed in 2008 dollars.

Table 4.12 presents the estimated equation. As before, all

are panel regressions estimated in first differences (changes in variables rather than levels, except for the dummy variable and the interaction term). The dependent variable is change in average household liabilities by quintile and year. The first three right-hand variables are the change in average income lagged one year, the year dummy variable, and the interaction term of income and the year dummy. The fourth right-hand variable is the change in the Theil index of income inequality. That is the variable of central interest because it is expected to capture the effect, if any, of income inequality upon changes in household liabilities.

The coefficient on the change in the Theil index is positive as expected (higher income inequality is associated with more household borrowing), but it is not statistically significant.

Turning to the other right-hand or independent variables, the change in income variable is positive as expected and highly significant. The year dummy is positive and insignificant. The interaction term is positive as expected and highly significant. The interaction term appears in the years 2004–07, when the change in liabilities was much higher than in earlier years.

This result by quintile and year provides weak support of the hypothesis that rising income inequality leads to rising household debt. The fact that the coefficient on the Theil index is not statistically significant is the main drawback. That may in part result from the small sample size, 110, compared with the state regression equations with sample sizes of 400 or more. Again, however, there is risk of the ecological fallacy because the observations are for *averages* of quintiles, not individual households. Future work on this issue would be markedly improved by using the individual household data from the Consumer Expenditure Survey.

V

Consumption Theory
and Its Critics

The neoclassical theory of consumption is not germane for understanding the financial crisis and the Great Recession. Jettisoning that theory in favor of one that gives central place to the distribution of income, relative income, and consumption, as well as household debt, is necessary for devising public policies to shorten the Great Recession by dealing with the huge overhang of household debt.

This chapter traces the development of the economic theory of consumption from Malthus and Ricardo to Milton Friedman. The arguments of critics of the prevailing Friedman–Modigliani–Brumberg paradigm are presented, leading to the outline of a theory to replace it. In the existing paradigm, there is no place for income distribution. Consequently, public policy analysis of the Great Recession leaves out of consideration what is a major cause of the Great Recession and the slow recovery.

The central concept of Pareto efficiency for economic theory renders income distribution unimportant. Also, Kuznets's hypothesis of eventually falling income inequality in rich democratic states, which was long under way in the United States when he wrote, was morally appealing in the Cold War, and the "no free lunch" message of Okun was sobering for liberals. Malthus and Ricardo disputed over effective demand and saving. Ricardo accepted Say's law (supply creates its own demand) while Malthus did not. Malthus believed that the distribution of income affected aggregate demand, and that excess saving by capitalists and landlords could lower demand. Under Say's law, that cannot happen in the aggregate economy because the act of production generates sufficient demand. Ricardo won that dispute in that classical economics followed his analysis based on Say's law. A century later, Keynes demurred. He argued that the *attempt* to save too much could lower output, income, and employment, thus reducing saving, too. Keynes was sympathetic to Malthus's view on effective demand and the importance of the distribution of income. He inferred from his analysis of the average and marginal propensity to consume that as aggregate income rises, the average propensity to consume (APC) falls. Thus in the long term, the economy would face slower growth or stagnation. To postpone such a development, Keynes believed that a more equal distribution of income would make effective demand stronger than a less equal distribution of income. Empirical evidence and new theories of consumption eclipsed Keynes's view on consumption. The post–World War II boom in the United States included a stable, not a falling, APC as incomes rose rapidly. Modigliani and Brumberg's theory of consumption argued that the APC was stable, and the empirical evidence appeared to confirm that. Income distribution played no role in their theory. Also excluded were psychological factors driving consumption that Keynes considered important. However, the theory of Modigliani and Brumberg does provide an explanation for the positive coupling of income inequality with a rising APC through their emphasis on wealth, although they did not anticipate that link.

The permanent income theory of consumption developed by Milton Friedman has become, along with the views of Modigliani and Brumberg, the mainstream view. Two of the three basic assumptions of his consumption theory no longer hold true—namely, a stable income distribution and a constant saving rate. The APC has *not* been stable, as Friedman assumed, but rather has risen for twenty-five years. Recent empirical work calls into question his view that income fluctuations are mostly confined to transitory income and thus do not affect consumption.

There are some modern critiques of the mainstream theory of consumption. They posit roles for income inequality and household debt in explaining consumption equality in the face of rising income inequality and the falling rate of saving. We consider both Veblen's and Frank's theories of consumption, in which emulation of the consumption of others looms large. Duesenberry's theory of consumption gives central place to relative income and consumption. Some behavioral economists have attacked the all-important rational consumer premise of mainstream consumption theory, resurrecting Keynes's psychological motives in consumption. We will consider the technical arguments as to whether the observed rise of the APC is real or not. Finally, we will look at a revised theory of consumption in which income distribution and consumer debt are central, and the rational consumer is replaced by a distribution of heterogeneous consumers whose choices are not always rational.

Pareto Efficiency, Kuznets's Inverted-U Hypothesis, and Okun's Tradeoff

"An economic situation is Pareto efficient if there is no way to make some group of people better off without making some other group of people worse off."[1] Pareto efficiency means that any change that leaves at least one person better off, and no person worse off, is an improvement. Applying the Pareto efficiency principle to the distribution of income, any change that raises the income of some while leaving the income of others unchanged is an improvement—that is, a rise in total utility. Thus an income increase that all goes to the top 1 percent of the income distribution (or the bottom 1 percent) is Pareto efficient. This principle of Pareto efficiency is a fundamental tenet of neoclassical economics. The historical distribution of income in industrialized nations mostly shows all groups with *absolute* gains. Such changes are Pareto efficient, and the *distribution* of gains is not an issue for positive economics. Hence economic theory has nothing to say about the distribution of income. "But efficiency is not the only goal of economic policy. For example, efficiency has almost nothing to say about income distribution or economic justice."[2]

But it was not just economic theory that turned economists' attention away from income distribution; it was also empirical evidence provided by Simon Kuznets.[3] Using historical data for a number of countries, Kuznets argued that in the shift from agricultural societies to industrialized societies, income inequality would rise rapidly because of growing concentration of industrial wealth. Eventually, with the expansion of democracy and institutions favoring economic protections for labor and a strong social safety net, income inequality would decrease from its peak in the period of rapid industrialization—thus the name, "Kuznets's inverted-U hypothesis." With time on the horizontal or x-axis and a measure of income inequality, such as the Gini coefficient, on the vertical or y-axis, the curve would rise (more inequality) in the rapid industrialization phase, then reach a peak, and begin to decline. His hypothesis gained wide attention and support in the post–World War II era of the United States because it seemed to trace the actual path of United States income inequality: rising in the Gilded Age, peaking in 1929, and declining during the Depression, World War II, and the postwar boom proceeding when Kuznets's hypothesis was promulgated during the 1950s and 1960s. It was a reassuring story favoring capitalism in the midst of the Cold War competition with communism. It is not, however, a story that has held up well, as income inequality has reversed course, rising for almost four decades.

Another reassuring story that gained much attention and respect was told by Arthur Okun, a liberal economist from Yale who had served in Democratic administrations, in his book *Equality and Efficiency: The Big Tradeoff* (1975).[4] The message was that gains in social welfare through progressive taxation could come only at the loss of efficiency, which would reduce economic growth and future living standards. Although Okun provided no strong evidence, his notion of a strict tradeoff took root in the policy world. It was already congenial to mainstream economists because of their belief in full employment, whereby the shift of resources to social goods necessarily meant fewer resources for private goods.

The centrality of Pareto efficiency in economics suggested that we need not worry about income inequality in theory because any redistribution of income that made some better off and others worse off was not Pareto efficient and so

was beyond the domain of positive economics. Kuznets's inverted-U hypothesis, supported empirically, suggested that we
need not worry about income inequality in fact because it was
destined to fall. Okun's tradeoff was a sober announcement to
liberals that there are "no free lunches." All that questionable
past baggage has been dragged into the present, resulting in
little interest in income distribution or inequality by mainstream economists. Counting articles published in the most
prestigious economic journals from 2009 through 2013, very
few are about income inequality or income distribution generally, based on their titles. The highest count, nine in those
five years, goes to the annual *American Economic Review Papers and Proceedings*. Seven of the nine, however, were in the
most recent annual for 2013. The regular *American Economic
Review* and the *Journal of Political Economy* are tied, with six
articles each. The *Quarterly Journal of Economics* comes in
last, with five articles over five years. That total of twenty-six
articles about income distribution or income inequality over
five years amounts to less than 2 percent of the 1,561 articles
published in those journals. That certainly indicates lack of
interest and perhaps some hostility. As Krugman noted in his
review of Thomas Piketty's book *Capital in the Twenty-first
Century,* "Some economists (not to mention politicians) tried
to shout down any mention of inequality at all. 'Of the tendencies that are harmful to sound economics, the most seductive, and in my opinion the most poisonous, is to focus
on questions of distribution,' declared Robert Lucas Jr. of the
University of Chicago, the most influential macroeconomist
of his generation, in 2004."[5] Although economic theory may
be silent about income distribution, macroeconomics, in its
incipient early phase before it was carved out as a subfield of
economics, did consider income distribution in its musings

about what we now call "effective demand." What those early writers had in mind was not the distribution of income among households as we mean by it today, but rather the distribution of factor payments between three groups: wages to laborers and profits to capitalists and landlords. In that simpler world of early nineteenth-century Britain, the groups demarked the "haves" were capitalists and landlords, and the "have-nots" were laborers. Thus it is not mistaken to read their remarks on the "distribution of product" as pertaining to the distribution of income.

The Malthus–Ricardo Dispute over Effective Demand

Say's law has been commonly stated as "supply creates its own demand." What Say actually wrote on a section dealing with demand in his *Treatise on Political Economy* (translated from French in 1824) is, first, "Which leads us to a conclusion, that may at first sight appear paradoxical; viz. that it is production which opens a demand for products." And second, "Thus the mere circumstance of the creation of one product immediately opens a vent for other products." And finally, "Thus, it is the aim of good government to stimulate production, of bad government to encourage consumption."[6]

Say's law was accepted by Ricardo.[7] As Cottrell points out, "the central thrust of the ideas that have been thus labeled [Say's law], in the writings of Say and Ricardo, is simple enough: there can be no such thing as a general deficiency of demand, although particular goods can obviously be overproduced in the sense of being produced in such quantities that they cannot be sold at their natural price."[8]

Malthus did not accept Say's law, as noted by Schumpeter: "A much more important reason for Malthus' dissent from Say and much more basic to his principle of effectual or effective demand was, however, his opinion that saving, even if promptly invested, may lead to a deadlock if carried beyond a certain optimal point."[9] In his biographical essay on Malthus, Keynes notes, "In economic discussions Ricardo was the abstract and *a priori* theorist, Malthus the inductive and intuitive investigator who hated to stray too far from what he could test by reference to the facts and his own intuition." Contrasting the two, largely based on their correspondence over many years, Keynes writes, "Ricardo is investigating the theory of the *distribution* of the product in conditions of equilibrium, and Malthus is concerned with what determines the *volume* of output day by day in the real world. Malthus is dealing with the monetary economy in which we happen to live; Ricardo with the abstraction of a neutral money economy."[10]

Although Malthus was not as clear in his writing as one would wish, in a letter to Ricardo he emphasizes the central importance of what we would call the distribution of income as well as discretionary or non-necessity consumption and the danger of excess saving: "But the grand question is whether it [total production] is distributed in such a manner between the different parties as to occasion the most effective demand for future produce: . . . an attempt to accumulate very rapidly which implies a considerable diminution of unproductive consumption by greatly impairing the usual motives to production must prematurely check the progress of wealth."[11] Keynes argues that the point about saving was made clearer in Malthus's *Principles of Political Economy* (1820) than in the correspondence with Ricardo, where Malthus addresses the slump in Britain following the end of the Napoleonic war: "He [Malthus] points out that the trouble was due to the diversion of resources, previously devoted to war, to the accumulation of savings; . . . and that public works and expenditure by land-lords and persons of property was the appropriate remedy."[12] Keynes argues that Malthus saw that saving is not necessarily a public virtue. Attempts to save could shrink total output. Keynes notes that in Malthus's preface to his *Principles of Political Economy*, he recognizes the importance of saving for the increase of production, but that too much saving could curb the growth of wealth. Ricardo disagreed. Keynes notes that "Surely it was a great fault in Ricardo to fail entirely to see any significance in this line of thought."[13]

The careful analysis of the Malthus–Ricardo debate by Allin Cottrell faults Malthus and argues that "Ricardo deserved to get the better of the debate."[14] Maybe so, but Ricardo did not struggle with the important issues of effective demand, and excess saving, issues that lay dormant in economics until Keynes's *General Theory of Employment, Interest and Money* (1936).

Keynes's Theory of Consumption

Keynes developed his theory of consumption in that book. Mostly expressed in words, it has been translated into algebra in generations of macroeconomics texts, a clarifying improvement made possible by the development of systems of national income accounts in developed nations after 1936. However, something was lost in the translation into algebra—namely, the importance of psychological factors in determining consumption. His key idea was that the marginal propensity to consume is positive and less than one, while the average propensity to consume falls as income rises. His controversial idea, in light of his classical economics predecessors and contemporaries, is that the rate of interest is relatively unimportant in determining consumption, whereas income is of central importance. His consumption function is:

$$C = a + bY,\qquad(1)$$

where C is aggregate consumption, Y is aggregate income, $a > 0$, and $0 < b < 1$ is the marginal propensity to consume. Dividing both sides by Y gives the average propensity to consume, APC.

$$APC = C/Y = a/Y + b\qquad(2)$$

This satisfies Keynes's condition that as income, Y, increases, the average propensity to consume falls. But the post–World War II economy of the United States did not satisfy Keynes's condition. That is, higher incomes after the war, induced by strong economic growth, did not result in a declining APC and thus a rise in the rate of saving. Thus the postwar experience did not support Keynes's contention that the APC falls as income rises: "Since I regard the propensity to consume as being (normally) as such to have a wider gap between income and consumption as income increases, it naturally follows that the collective propensity for the community as a whole may depend . . . on the distribution of incomes within it."[15]

Although Keynes doesn't explicitly state "average propensity to consume," his definition of "propensity to consume" in the *General Theory* clearly means the average, not the marginal.[16] What is unclear is if he meant that the long-term APC of the nation falls as income rises, which Kuznets showed not to be the case, or that the cross section of APC in any year across income groups falls with rising income. He may have meant both, in which case he was only half wrong.[17]

Recent time-series data that contradict Keynes expec-

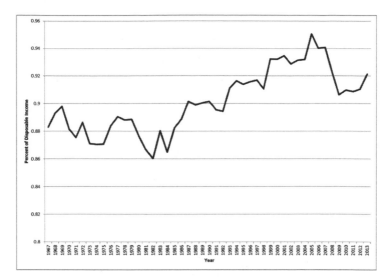

Figure 5.1. Average propensity to consume (APC), 1967–2013. *Sources:* Council of Economic Advisers (2011), Table B-30, and Bureau of Economic Analysis (n.d.), "National Economic Accounts," July 2014.

tation are shown in Figure 5.1. There the line is the average propensity to consume calculated from aggregate personal consumption expenditures and disposable income, 1967–2013. Rather than decline over those forty-six years, it oscillates between a ceiling of 0.90 (1969) and a floor of 0.86 (1982) from 1967 to 1986. Thereafter it rises for twenty years, except in recessions, hitting a peak of 0.95 in 2005. That pattern of a long-term *rise* of the APC was not anticipated by Keynes, and certainly not by Friedman or Modigliani and Brumberg.

Modigliani and Brumberg's Theory of Consumption

Modigliani and Brumberg were aware of the fact that the long-term data of stable APC did not agree with the short-term data of falling APC.[18] Their life-cycle hypothesis solved that anomaly by replacing current income with lifetime income and by introducing wealth, accumulated through saving, in the consumption function. The rational consumer saves while working and dissaves when retired with the object of maintaining stable consumption over the consumer's expected lifetime. Their consumption function for the economy, as represented in the currently popular macroeconomics text by Mankiw, is

$$C = \alpha W + \beta Y, \tag{3}$$

where W is accumulated wealth and Y is income. For simplicity of exposition, the growth path of W and Y as well as the effect of the interest rate on W are omitted. The graph of this consumption function for individuals in a given year is a straight line where the intercept is αW. The average propensity to consume is derived by dividing the consumption function by Y.

$$APC = C/Y = \alpha(W/Y) + \beta \tag{4}$$

This formulation solves the anomaly of the short-run and the long-run APC, as Mankiw explains: "Because wealth does not vary proportionately with income from person to person or year to year, we should find that high income corresponds to a low average propensity to consume when looking at data across individuals or over short periods of time. But, over long periods of time, wealth and income grow together, resulting in a constant ratio W/Y and thus a constant average propensity to consume."[19] Contrary to the views of Modigliani and Brumberg, the APC might rise over a long period, as it did from 1984 to 2005. A theory that can explain those long-term increases in the APC lies in Modigliani and Brumberg's analy-

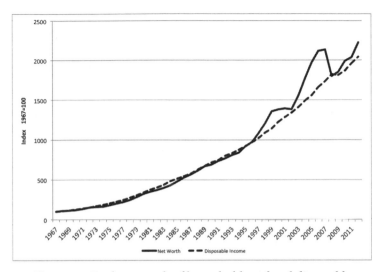

Figure 5.2. Real net worth of households and real disposable income. Dotted line: Disposable income. Solid line: Net worth. *Source:* Bureau of Economic Analysis (n.d.), "National Economic Accounts," Table S.3.a, December 2013.

sis of consumption in which the importance of wealth for consumption is asserted. Examining equation (4), it is clear that APC will rise if wealth, W, grows faster than income, Y, for a long period, and if $\acute{a} > 0$. As shown in Figure 5.2, real net worth of households has been expanding faster than real disposable income from the mid-1990s until 2007, except for the sharp drop when the high-tech stock market bubble burst in 2000. It would be a stretch to call that twelve-year pattern "temporary."

Figure 5.3 plots the W/Y term of the Modigliani APC, using net worth as W and disposable income as Y. As shown, W/Y edged up from 4.4 in 1974 to 5.0 in 1994, a gain of 0.6 points in two decades. In the next five years, 1994–99, it shot up 1.5 points, to 6.5. Then it tumbled in the tech bubble and

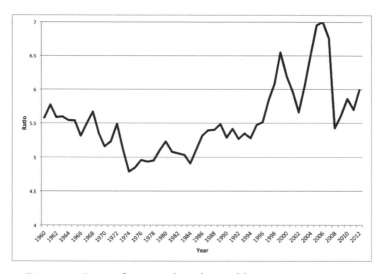

Figure 5.3. Ratio of net worth to disposable income, 1960–2012.
Source: Bureau of Economic Analysis (n.d.), "National Economic
Accounts," Table S.3.a, December 2013.

rebounded in the housing bubble to a high of 6.7 in 2006 before dropping to 5.0 in 2009. In the thirty-two years from 1974 to 2006, W/Y rose 2.3 points, contrary to Mankiw's assertion, cited above, that "over long periods of time, wealth and income grow together, resulting in a constant ratio W/Y and thus a constant average propensity to consume."[20]

The expression for APC based on Modigliani and Brumberg's consumption function, equation (4), can be used to explain the long-term rise of the APC (see Figure 5.1). Clearly, wealth grew faster than income (shown in Figure 5.2), and so by equation (4) APC would rise, as it did. That is not an empirical result expected by Modigliani and Brumberg. Likewise, they posited no role for income distribution in their theory of consumption.

As shown, increasing income inequality and a rising

APC occurred together in the period 1984–2005. But what is the theory that would support such a causal link? Faced with rising income inequality, households may attempt to maintain consumption through increased borrowing. In the face of a "hard income constraint," consumption limited by income, such attempts would not be successful. But a "soft income constraint" enables households to maintain or increase consumption through increased borrowing. As indicated in Chapter IV, household indebtedness across all income quintiles expanded much more than income from 1995 to 2007. Because the largest part of their increased indebtedness was for residential property, that borrowing enhanced their wealth as house prices rose during the bubble. Hence, income inequality indirectly contributed to the faster rise of wealth than income.

Friedman's Theory of Consumption and Some Critics

Friedman, like Modigliani and Brumberg, rejected Keynes's formulation that consumption depends on current income.[21] Friedman hypothesized that annual income of a person or household consisted of two parts: permanent income and transitory income. Rationality would require that the consumer would base consumption only upon permanent income. Thus Friedman's consumption function states that consumption is some fraction of permanent income, Y^p, noted by Mankiw as

$$C = \alpha Y^p \tag{5}$$

Then Mankiw shows the APC in Friedman's model as

$$APC = C/Y = \alpha Y^p/Y \tag{6}$$

And he notes, "According to the permanent-income hypothesis, the average propensity to consume depends on the ratio of permanent income [Y^p] to current income [Y]. When current income temporarily rises above permanent income, the average propensity to consume temporarily falls; when current income temporarily falls below permanent income, the average propensity to consume temporarily rises."[22]

In Friedman's theory of consumption, the rational consumer plans *permanent* consumption based on permanent income. For one consumer, the propensity to consume out of permanent income is a function of the rate of interest, ratio of wealth to permanent income, and household characteristics, such as age and family size. When Friedman generalizes individual consumption to aggregate consumption, he assumes that the "distribution of consumer units by income is independent of their distribution by (i), w, and u [rate of interest, ratio of wealth to permanent income, and household characteristics]."[23] So his aggregate consumption function has permanent consumption a linear function of permanent income,

$$C^p = k \ (Y^p), \tag{7}$$

where the coefficient k is determined by the myriad factors noted above for millions of households. But he recognizes that "The assumption . . . that the distribution of consumer units by income is independent of their distribution by (i), w, and u is obviously false in a descriptive sense." Nonetheless, he asserts in the same paragraph,

> At the same time, although the interdependence
> between these variables and the distribution of income may be important for some problems, it may

> not be for this aggregation. The interdependence
> enters in a rather complex way and equation (2.10)
> [equation (7) above] is a good approximation even
> when interdependence exists. . . . If . . . equation
> (2.10) [7] is a good approximation of the relation
> among observed magnitudes, this must be inter-
> preted to mean that the interdependence is of only
> secondary importance.[24]

That is a critical assumption because it removes the "distribution of consumer units by income" as a determinant of the
APC and thus the saving rate. Thus Friedman's k, the APC, is
constant in the long run, and therefore so is the saving rate.

The development of Friedman's theory of consumption
by mainstream economists uses a "representative agent" to
stand for the millions of heterogeneous consumer units. The
intellectual trend to establish micro foundations for macroeconomics, championed by Lucas, has failed to displace the
representative agent from macro models of consumption and
saving. Although one writer, Kevin Hoover, states of mainstream macroeconomists that "most have accepted micro
foundations in the form of the representative agent model or
some near variant, despite the fact that a plausible case has
never been offered for how any such agent could legitimately
represent millions of economic decision makers."[25]

In a paper comparing representative agent models, the
mainstream approach, with consumer heterogeneity models,
the authors conclude:

> In representative agent models with time additive
> preferences, it seems difficult to obtain the departure
> from permanent income behavior that we observe

in the incomplete markets models with heterogeneous preferences. In other words, the interaction
of consumers with heterogeneous preferences in an
incomplete-market setting leads to new insights.
Among the models we study, those that come clos-
est to matching real-world wealth distributions are
precisely models with heterogeneous preferences
and incomplete markets. . . . As we have shown in
this paper, introducing preference heterogeneity
into the standard model allows a closer match between the model and data.[26]

In the concluding section of his book *A Theory of the Consumption Function* (1957), Friedman takes issue with the inter-
pretations attached to the Keynesian theory of consumption
—namely, that the APC will decline over time as income rises.
He asserts instead, "Yet there is ample evidence that (a) inequality of income has, if anything, decreased over time in
the United States, (b) savings have been a roughly constant
fraction of income over time in the United States, (c) computed regressions have steadily been higher, the later the date
of the budget study. All three observations are entirely consistent with the permanent income hypothesis presented in this
monograph."[27] His first two observations, declining income
inequality and stable saving rate (which infers a stable APC),
are not true for the period 1984–2007 (see Table 2.2 and Figure
5.1), and also not true for the early twentieth century, as shown
in Chapter VI. His third observation is based on regression
equations relating consumption to income in real dollars that
he estimated using data from eight budget studies ranging
over the long period from 1888–90 to 1950. He claims that
those regression equations show that "computed regressions

have steadily been higher, the later the date of the budget study." That is, calculated consumption rises with later budget studies, contrary to the view that "regressions computed from budget studies made at widely spaced dates will not differ systematically."[28] Friedman does not show the estimated regression equations that he used to calculate the real consumption levels.

Friedman's period of analysis, pre-1957, was mostly one of falling income inequality, except for the 1920s (which he overlooked), so he had no reason to ask the question of whether income inequality leads to consumption inequality. In light of the long rise of income inequality, the question is now germane, and it is posed by Dirk Krueger and Fabrizio Perri in an empirical and theoretical article. In a careful analysis of Consumer Expenditure Survey data, they find that rising income inequality has not been accompanied by a similar rise of consumption inequality. In their theoretical model, maintaining stable consumption in the face of increasing income inequality may be facilitated by credit and insurance—in other words, by a soft budget constraint. "If, however, the structure of private financial markets and informal insurance arrangements does not respond to changes in the underlying stochastic income process of individuals, then no further hedging against the increasing risk is possible, and the increase in income inequality leads to a more pronounced rise in consumptions inequality."[29] In other words, if consumers face a hard budget constraint. They present a figure in which the Gini coefficient is plotted against non-secured consumer credit as a share of disposable income. It shows the two moving upward in tandem from the late 1960s to the early 2000s. They conclude, "Combining this figure with our consumption inequality observations may suggest that consumers could, and in fact did, make stronger use of credit markets exactly when they needed to (starting in the mid-1970s), in order to insulate consumption from bigger income fluctuations."[30]

Those authors in the Friedman mainstream tradition (Krueger and Perri) thus assert that rising income inequality leads to increased consumer borrowing, a major proposition of this book. But in their case, such borrowing is only temporary, in order to smooth consumption. As shown in Chapter IV, the massive rise of household debt cannot be described as temporary.

The empirical part of their paper, covering 1980–2003, convincingly shows that even with the large rise of income inequality in the United States, consumption inequality has risen very little. The theoretical part of their paper hypothesizes that "the volatility of idiosyncratic labour income has been an important factor in the increase in income inequality."[31] What they mean by "idiosyncratic labour income" is transitory income. So the implication is that the rise of income inequality is all in the transitory component, not in the permanent component. That is simply an assertion with no empirical support. Without that assertion, income inequality would have to be recognized as affecting permanent income, contradicting Friedman's view. Permanent consumption is protected or maintained through borrowing, and Krueger and Perri protect Friedman's permanent income hypothesis by assuming the rise of income inequality is almost all in the transitory component. That assumption is called into question by van Treeck, who cites a number of works that provide statistical evidence of increased variance of permanent income, not transitory income. "These results seem to conflict with the view that the rise in inequality was driven by insurable temporary shocks over the 1990s."[32]

A paper that is strongly empirical, utilizing a vast Social Security database going back to 1937, reaches the opposite conclusion from Krueger and Perri. "In particular we find that increases in annual earnings inequality are driven almost entirely by increases in permanent earnings inequality, with much more modest changes in the variability of transitory earnings."[33]

Another author also links income inequality to rising household debt and stable consumption inequality. Matteo Iacoviello shows that income inequality and the debt of households move together. Measuring inequality with the cross section standard deviation of log earnings, he finds that it was stable from 1963 to 1980 and rose sharply thereafter. Household debt as a percentage of disposable income follows a quite similar path, rising from 66 percent of disposable income in 1981 to 113 percent in 2003, the last year for his data. He develops a dynamic general equilibrium model to explain the trend and cycle in household debt. He concludes, "The rise of income inequality of the 1980s and 1990s can, at the same time, account for the increase in household debt, the large widening of wealth inequality, and the relative stability of consumption inequality." Similar to Krueger and Perri, he finds that expanded use of credit prevents a rise of consumption inequality when income inequality increases. "In the model presented here, the mechanism through which consumption inequality rises less than income inequality in [sic] an expansion of credit from the rich to the poor."[34]

For this study, income inequality and consumption inequality measures have been calculated—namely, standard deviations from the relative distribution of aggregate after-tax income and aggregate consumption for the CEX data by quintile for selected years from 1984 to 2007. The income standard deviations are much larger, 46 percent to 58 percent larger, than the consumption standard deviations, indicating that income inequality is much larger than consumption inequality. This agrees with the findings of both Krueger and Perri and Iacoviello.

More Doubts About Friedman's Consumption Theory: Rajan, Van Treeck, and Others

Recent writers challenge Friedman on a number of issues in his theory of consumption. One, that relative income, not absolute income, is of central importance because households care about their relative standing.[35] Two, that saving *rates* across income classes are not stable but rather they increase with income.[36] Three, that rising earnings inequality is *not* driven by fluctuations in transitory earnings but rather by rises in permanent earnings inequality.[37] Four, the assumed "hard intertemporal budget constraint, does not adequately describe household spending and borrowing decisions in the past quarter century . . . with financial innovation and greater access to debt, the year-by-year budget constraint has become soft."[38] Five (and not recent), that the APC is independent of the level of permanent income.[39]

In his book *Fault Lines,* Raghuram Rajan also ties rising income inequality to rising consumer borrowing that became unsustainable and brought on the financial crash. But in making the link from income inequality to rising household borrowing, he indirectly undermined the permanent income hypothesis of Friedman by arguing that the massive rise of household debt was unsustainable. In Friedman's model, debt was a temporary recourse to smooth consumption over periods of lower transitory income. "I have argued that an important political response to inequality was populist credit expansion, which allowed people the consumption possibilities that their stagnant incomes otherwise could not support."[40]

Here is a paraphrase of what van Treeck calls the "Rajan hypothesis." The benefits of rising aggregate income over past decades have been confined to a small set of households at the top of the income distribution, so that consumption of lower groups has been financed through rising use of credit. The process was facilitated by government directly through credit promotion and indirectly through deregulation of the financial sector. But with the drop of housing prices and the subprime mortgage crisis beginning in 2007, overindebtedness of the household sector became apparent and debt-financed private demand expansion ended. What van Treeck draws from Rajan's argument was not stated by Rajan but may be implied:

> The more important implication of his analysis is the rejection of the conventional theories of consumption, which see no link between the inequality of (permanent) income and aggregate personal consumption, and hence no need for government action to stimulate consumption and jobs in response to higher inequality. . . . The Rajan hypothesis posits that given the rise in inequality the credit expansion in the personal sector was both necessary for supporting aggregate demand and employment, and it was unsustainable. . . . This lack of attention to inequality seemed justified by the permanent income hypothesis . . . which posits that household consumption is unrelated to the inequality of permanent income. . . . The Rajan hypothesis, which relies on the assumption of a higher

> inequality in the permanent component of income,
> is thus of great theoretical importance, and it bears
> resemblance to the relative income hypothesis.[41]

This following quote from van Treeck may be reading too much into Rajan, but it underscores the importance of relative income: "Rather, the Rajan hypothesis can be seen as an application of the relative income hypothesis, which predicts that households will react to a decline in (permanent) relative income by lower saving and higher debt."[42]

Two recent authors, Michael Bordo and Christopher Meissner, take issue with both Rajan and with Michael Kumhof, Romain Ranciere, and Pablo Winant because they "propose that rising inequality led to a credit boom and eventually to a financial crisis in the United States in the first decade of the 21st century as it did in the 1920s." In their econometric analysis, they examine data from 1920 through 2000 for fourteen advanced nations and conclude, "Credit booms heighten the probability of a banking crisis, but we find no evidence that a rise in top income shares leads to credit booms."[43]

Tuomas Malinen criticizes the econometrics of the Bordo and Meissner article: "As real income keeps on stagnating, credit acquired by lower income households keeps on growing and this trend eventually leads to defaults and stress among financial institutions. First differencing removes this trend and focuses the analysis on the short-term effects of inequality on credit. If the relationship between inequality and credit is long-run, i.e., trending in nature, using first differenced variables may give biased information."[44] His panel econometric results lead him to conclude: "In this study we have tested the existence of such a long-run relationship [between income inequality and the share of credit to income].

According to the results, there is a long-run steady-state relationship between income inequality and leverage in developed economies. The long-run elasticity of leverage with respect to income inequality was found to be positive. This indicates that income inequality increases leverage in the economy."[45] In an article by Christopher Brown that asks whether income distribution matters for effective demand, simulations are presented by income deciles for the United States in 2001. His first-order autoregressive equation for aggregate consumption includes the Theil index of income inequality on the right-hand side. When he does a simulation at Theil = 0.14 and then Theil = 0, perfect equality of income, the resulting rise in consumption is only 1 percent. Then he does simulations where Theil = 0.14 in both cases, but in one he imposes a hard income constraint—that is, consumption by quintile cannot be greater than income, and not in the other. With the hard income constraint, aggregate consumption drops almost 16 percent. "The results indicate that, if income imposes a hard constraint on spending, income distribution can have very significant implications for effective demand."[46] He notes the importance of widened credit availability in the past few decades. "Thus widened credit availability is comparable to a decrease in income inequality in terms of its effects upon the propensity to consume. It follows that the aggregate propensity to consume can remain stable or even increase, amidst a sharp rise in income inequality—given a sufficient surge in borrowing."[47] As shown in Figure 5.1, the APC has increased in a period of rising income inequality made possible by a surge in borrowing.

One of the key assumptions of Friedman's permanent income hypothesis is that the APC is stable over time. By definition, if the APC is stable over time, then so too is the saving rate, which is equal to 1 – APC, a stability that Friedman notes in his conclusion. But the personal saving rate in the United States has been trending down. Prior to 1984 it was fluctuating around 10 percent. Thereafter it mostly declined, reaching a low of 3 percent in 2005 (see Figure 4.1). Neither the permanent income hypothesis nor the life-cycle hypothesis can explain the long decline in the saving rate (the inverse of the long rise in the APC), as one Friedman critic, David Bunting, notes. He seeks the explanation for the drop in the U.S. saving rate in the distribution of income, which is usually ignored. Making use of income distribution series of both CEX and CPS, he combines quintiles one and two into the low-income group, quintiles three and four into the middle-income group, and quintile five into the high-income group, and then analyzes the saving behavior by each group from the mid-1980s until 2005. Bunting concludes:

> As the distribution data clearly shows, since 1980 saving by high income households accounts for not the bulk, but all of aggregate saving. . . . Representing 20 percent of households, the high income group saving rates have remained virtually unchanged since 1985–87. . . . On the other hand, undetected in the aggregate data, both the saving rates and the saving of the lowest 80 percent of households has deteriorated since 1985–87 as the low income group rates fell 30 percent or more while dissaving increased by $360 billion and the middle income group saving collapsed with both saving rates and saving turning from positive to negative figures.[48]

He argues that the saving rate should be calculated as a weighted average rather than assuming that the aggregate rate represents all behavior. The use of the aggregate rate to represent all consumers implies that saving is unaffected by poverty or affluence and that the distribution of income does not matter.

In an earlier article, Bunting is more explicit in faulting Friedman as well as Modigliani and Brumberg for using a representative agent as reflecting aggregate consumption behavior: "Unfortunately, by reducing aggregate spenders to one, it [assumption of a representative agent] had the great disadvantage of precluding consideration of any distributional and demographic influences on aggregate behavior because with only one agent, income as well as age, race, or sex differences are meaningless."[49] The critics noted above are of course not the only critics of the neoclassical theory of consumption. That puts them in the company of Malthus and Keynes and in opposition to Ricardo and the neoclassical synthesis, which has as one of its major tenets the theory of consumption developed by Friedman and also by Modigliani and Brumberg, who hold the view, by omission, that income distribution does not matter for a theory of consumption and saving. Their criticisms, as well as those of Veblen, Duesenberry, and the behavioral economists, are central to the theme of this chapter.

Veblen and Frank

Up to this point the parts of this chapter are mostly chronological: before and after Friedman. Here that pattern is broken by introducing Thorstein Veblen, who wrote long before Friedman. The reason for this departure is that Veblen can be considered a forerunner of behavioral economics.

Veblen, an economist classified in the Institutionalist School, wrote in the late nineteenth and early twentieth century. At that time there were no good data available on income distribution or aggregate consumption in the United States. His major works, however, present a theory of consumption and have implications for income distribution. Conspicuous consumption of the rich, he argued, would stimulate emulation by the non-rich. In *The Theory of Business Enterprise,* he postulated a clash between engineers and professionals with businessmen who seek to maximize return. He thought the former were interested in technical improvements for raising output and lowering price, while the latter, businessmen, sought to limit output and raise price. The first, he argued, would lead to full employment and high wages, while the second to unemployment and low wages. The implication for income distribution is clear.[50] His *Theory of the Leisure Class* was enormously popular, especially during the Great Depression, when he was lionized: "The collapse of orthodox economic doctrine during the years of the world depression has vindicated the keenly analytic and prophetic writings of Thorstein Veblen."[51] But he never made much impression on mainstream (neoclassical) economics. In Joseph Schumpeter's magisterial *History of Economic Analysis,* first published in 1954, the index notes four page references to Veblen. All of them are incidental asides. None notes his challenge to the pre-Friedman neoclassical theory of consumption.[52] To be fair to Schumpeter, his title is *History of Economic Analysis,* not history of economic thought. Because Veblen produced no analytical models or empirical support for his theories, we can presume that Schumpeter did not include him among his parade of economists. Obscurity was no barrier to inclusion, just as fame was no assurance of inclusion.

Veblen's influence apparently lives on. In an empirical paper, "Emulation, Inequality, and Work Hours: Was Thorstein Veblen Right?" the authors, Bowles and Park, define "Veblen effects" as "the manner in which a desire to emulate the consumption standards of the rich may influence an individual's allocation of time between labor and leisure." The authors develop a model of the "Veblen effects" that they estimate econometrically for many OECD nations. They conclude: "We have shown that increased inequality induces people to work longer hours and have also provided evidence that the underlying cause is the Veblen effect of the consumption of the rich on the behavior of those less well off."[53] The mainstream consumption theory cannot countenance a "Veblen effect" because preferences are assumed independent—that is, no one cares what those better off are consuming.

One of Veblen's challenges to mainstream economics appeared in one of the profession's preeminent journals, then and now, the *Quarterly Journal of Economics,* entitled "Why Is Economics Not an Evolutionary Science?" In the first paragraph he complained, "It may be taken as the consensus of those men who are doing the serious work of modern anthropology, ethnology, and psychology, as well as those in the biological sciences proper, that economics is hopelessly behind the times, and unable to handle its subject matter in a way to entitle it to standing as a modern science."[54] More than a hundred years after Veblen wrote that, Robert Frank argued in his 2011 book, *The Darwin Economy,* that in a hundred years almost all economists would claim Darwin as the father of economics rather than Adam Smith. "One century hence, if a roster of professional economists is asked to identify the intellectual father of their discipline, a majority will name Charles Darwin."[55] In other words, Frank, like Veblen, thought that economics would become an evolutionary science. However, in Veblen's case it was a hope, while in Frank's case it is his optimistic perception of how economics is evolving. His reviewer in the *Journal of Economic Literature* (2012) was kind but dismissive, wondering if reading it was "an efficient use" of economists' time.[56]

Frank's case for Darwin replacing Smith as the intellectual parent of economics is that Darwin's definition of competition includes cases where it is good for the individual but bad for society and where it is good for both, whereas Smith's definition of competition (dumbed-down by libertarians) is good for the individual *and* good for society in *all* cases. Why does it matter? If the libertarians are right, there is no need for government regulation. If the Darwinians are right, then regulation can improve social outcomes. If the libertarians (read mainstream economists) are right, then absolute quantities (as in absolute income and absolute consumption) matter, not relative. If the Darwinians are right, then relative ranking and relative strength matter, not absolute. Without going into detail, prisoner's dilemmas and arms races are cases where individual rational choices doom the individual or the society. Only collective control can improve the outcome. The mainstream theory of consumption developed by Friedman as well as by Modigliani and Brumberg is based on rational actors making choices about absolute income and absolute consumption. But evidence indicates that real actors respond to relative income and relative consumption.

Duesenberry and the Behavioral Economists

James Duesenberry's book *Income, Saving and the Theory of Consumer Behavior* was published in 1949, eight years before Friedman's *Theory of the Consumption Function*. The key point he argues there is that consumer preferences are *not* independent, as assumed in the neoclassical model of consumer behavior ascribed to by Friedman as well as Modigliani and Brum-berg. That tenet of independence is held in spite of evidence from psychology and sociology to the contrary. Recall that Veblen, too, had criticized economics for ignoring the evidence of other social sciences.[57] Duesenberry cites facts to support his argument that preferences are interdependent. For example, "Thirty years ago [1911] the average urban family with a $1,500 income in 1940 prices saved 8 percent of its income. In 1941 a similarly placed family saved nothing. One can hardly argue that the desire for saving, whatever its source, had diminished in that period. For some reason, the forces leading to higher consumption increased during that period."[58] He stressed that the "fact that the attainment of a higher standard of living as an end in itself is a major social goal has great significance for the theory of consumption." The utility index of a person "depends not on the absolute level of his consumption, but on the ratio of his expenditures to those of other people. . . . Current consumption standards or desires are influenced by other peoples' consumption behavior." If preferences are interdependent, as he argues, then "low income groups are affected by the consumption of high income groups but not vice versa." That point was made by Veblen in 1899.

Relying on data for household saving, Duesenberry argued that the rational saver of the neoclassical model was not to be found among most consumers. "About 75 percent of spending units save virtually nothing. Most of these families will not be influenced in their saving by changes in interest rates, income expectations, or even by changes in their own preference parameters. . . . At (relatively) low levels of income, desires for current consumption are so strong that they overcome all considerations of the future." And further on saving, "The propensity to save of an individual can be regarded as a rising function of his percentile position in the income distribution."

In the conclusion, Duesenberry states, "The theory of saving just summarized is based on the assumption that consumers' preferences are interdependent and irreversible. Our theory of the relation between income and saving really depends on the validity of a single hypothesis, viz: that the utility index is a function of relative rather than absolute consumption expenditure."[59] His views (1) that preferences are interdependent and (2) that one's utility or satisfaction or happiness depends on relative consumption fly in the face of mainstream neoclassical consumption theory. It is an early expression of the behavioral economics view on consumption. That is why noted behavioral economist Robert Frank has labeled Duesenberry the first behavioral economist. About the reception of economists to Duesenberry's views, Frank has written: "Still, it is perhaps an understatement to say that the economics profession as a whole has shown little interest in the idea that people are deeply concerned about their relative standing in hierarchies. Duesenberry's theory of consumption behavior, for example, was quickly relegated to history-footnote status as soon as alternative theories appeared."[60] A recent econometric analysis provides empirical support to Duesenberry's claim that consumer preferences are interdependent. "I conclude that the negative effect of neighbors' earnings on well-being is real and that it is most likely caused by a psychological externality, that is, people having utility functions that depend on relative consumption in addition to absolute consumption."[61]

The optimizing rational consumer of the Friedman as well as the Modigliani and Brumberg models, models that have become the mainstream for consumption theory, are devoid of motives and proclivities we recognize as broadly shared, such as maintaining status in the perceived peer group, determining to save more, to lose weight, to stop smoking, next year but not now. A model that purports to explain behavior of consumers in facing choices about consumption and saving ignores what we all know about human behavior. Behavioral economist Robert Frank and his co-author Seth Levine do not ignore such behavior in their analysis of consumption. "Changes in one group's spending shifts the frame of reference that defines consumption standards for others just below them on the income scale, giving rise to expenditure cascades." They develop a model based on Duesenberry's relative income hypothesis. Using data for fifty states and the one hundred most populous counties, they find "evidence that rapid income growth concentrated among top earners in recent decades has stimulated a cascade of additional expenditure by those with lower earnings."[62] They argue that such cascades caused the drop in savings shown in Figure 4.1.

In another work, Frank criticizes Friedman's emphasis on absolute rather than relative income. He argues that empirical work shows that people care about their relative economic standing, not their absolute income.

> Strangest of all, Friedman's theory assumes that context has absolutely no effect on judgements about living standards. . . . In light of abundant evidence that context matters, it seems fair to say that Duesenberry's theory rests on a more realistic model of human nature than Friedman's. . . . Under the relative income hypothesis, for example, it is easy to understand why a majority of families experience significant retrenchments in living standards when they retire. Under the permanent income hypoth-

esis, this observation is a jarring anomaly. And yet
Duesenberry's relative income hypothesis is no
longer even mentioned in leading textbooks.[63]

Another notable behavioral economist who has criticized
mainstream consumption theory is George Akerlof. Incorpo-
rating true behavior, as George Akerlof asserted in his Nobel
acceptance speech, "Macroeconomics would then no longer
suffer from the 'ad hockery' of the neoclassical synthesis,
which had overridden the emphasis in *The General Theory*
on the role of psychological and sociological factors, such as
cognitive bias, reciprocity, fairness, herding, and social status.
My dream was to strengthen macroeconomic theory by in-
corporating assumptions honed to the observations of such
behavior."[64]

Akerlof points out that that one widely known phenomena the New Classical economics (rigorous successor to the
neoclassical synthesis), dominant now in macroeconomics,
cannot explain is chronic undersaving for retirement. "In the
New Classical model, individuals decide how much to consume and to save to maximize an intertemporal utility function. The consequence is that privately determined saving
should be just about optimal. But individuals commonly report disappointment with their saving behavior and, absent
social insurance programs, it is widely believed that most people would undersave. 'Forced saving' programs are extremely
popular." In his conclusion, Akerlof anoints Keynes as a behavioral economist.

Keynes' General Theory was the greatest contri-
bution to behavioral economics before the present
era. Almost everywhere Keynes blamed market

failures on psychological propensities (as in consumption) and irrationalities (as in stock market speculation). Immediately after its publication, the economics profession tamed Keynesian economics. They domesticated it as they translated it into the "smooth" mathematics of classical economics. But economies, like lions, are wild and dangerous.[65]

Is the APC Really Rising?

If the permanent income hypothesis is accepted, how would we interpret Figure 5.1, the actual APC for the United States over the past four decades? The APC rose from 0.88 in 1985 to a peak of 0.95 in 2005. That conforms to the theoretical case where current income falls below permanent income, but the actual case can hardly be described as "temporary" with the upward trend persisting for two decades. It could be objected that the APC of Figure 5.1 is calculated from annual real disposable income and consumption rather than Friedman's notion of permanent income. An approximation of the APC from permanent income frequently used is a four- or five-year moving average of income and consumption. Comparing a four-year moving average of the APC with the annual APC of Figure 5.1 does not show much difference. Instead of rising +0.068 from 1985 to 2005, the moving average rises +0.064. The long-term rise of the APC does not disappear when one uses an approximation of permanent income.

If that rise of APC is claimed to reflect increased income inequality, Friedman would not have agreed. "Empirical data show no tendency for inequality of income to increase. If anything, inequality seems to have been decreasing in recent decades."[66] Of course the recent long-term rise of income inequality was not under way when he wrote. Also, the drop in the APC from 0.95 in 2005 to just under 0.91 in 2009 implies that current income temporarily rose above permanent income, an unlikely scenario in this recent severe recession. Chapter VI returns to this issue in reviewing Kuznets's long-term data on the APC.

Mainstream macroeconomists have certainly noticed the observed rise of the APC, and the falling saving rate, since the mid-1980s. Most of the attention in the literature has been focused upon the falling rate of saving. For example, in an International Monetary Fund working paper addressing the decline of the saving rate, the authors identify causal factors that are all on the supply side: decreasing interest rates, financial liberalization, and increased housing liquidity.[67] No demand-side factors are considered. But the interesting question is not why the saving rate declined, but why the APC rose. The arguments of Duesenberry and Bunting noted above suggest that for most consumers, saving is a residual, the tail wagged by the consumption dog.

The question of whether the APC (now referred to in the literature as the consumption-income ratio) has been *really* rising turns on the technical issue of whether the ratio is stationary (no trend) or nonstationary (a trend). According to Friedman, the ratio is stationary—that is, the APC is stable over long periods. The only rigorous test for stationarity of a time-series variable is what is called a unit root test in econometrics. In one article, Steven Cook calculates different unit root tests than others have used for twenty OECD nations. He finds support for a stationary consumption-income ratio (APC) in all twenty nations. In another article, the authors, Eftymios Tsionas and Dmitris Christopoulos, calculate unit root tests for fourteen European nations' consumption-income ratios.

Eight of the fourteen turn out to be nonstationary (rejecting the Friedman claim), while six turn out to be stationary (not rejecting the Friedman claim).[68] The United States was not included in either study.

We have performed a unit root test for the APC data for the United States, 1967–2013, represented in Figure 5.1. The test we used is the common augmented Dickey-Fuller test. The test results indicate that the APC is nonstationary (rejecting the Friedman claim). That is, the test results support the view that the APC does have a trend. Our eyes did not fool us in this case.

Outline of a Revised Theory of Consumption

The analysis of aggregate consumption should begin with recognition of the centrality of income distribution for long-term saving and consumption. As shown above, the APC and, therefore, the saving rate can have long periods in which they are *not* stable: the APC moves up and the saving rate moves down. The reason that can happen and persist is that consumers choose to maintain consumption when confronted with rising income inequality.[69] They can succeed in that effort by reducing saving and increasing borrowing. On borrowing, Rajan argues that the government eases restrictions on borrowing as an offset to rising income inequality.[70] In a sensible world, consumer borrowing would be directed to buying assets expected to appreciate and thus aid in maintaining their consumption. That is exactly what they did, as explained in Chapter IV on debt (see Tables 4.5 and 4.6). The Modigliani and Brumberg APC equation, (4), shows that APC can rise if wealth grows faster than income, which it did for most of the period 1995–2007 (Figure 5.2). But maintaining consumption through reduced saving and increased borrowing to acquire appreciating assets is not sustainable in the long run. The rapid rise in wealth can be the result of a speculative bubble, as in the high-tech boom and in the housing boom. A revised theory of consumption must take such factors into consideration. It must also replace the representative rational consumer of Friedman, Modigliani, and Brumberg facing complete markets (insurance for every risk), with a realistic distribution of consumers with heterogeneous preferences by income, age, race, and so on subject to rational choices (buying appreciating assets early) as well as irrational choices (buying appreciating assets late) and facing incomplete markets (some risks not insurable). Looking back to Keynes and to behavioral economics can inform the effort to develop a revised theory of consumption. A revised theory may be messy, inelegant, and ugly. The current theory is tidy, elegant, and beautiful, but it is only true some of the time.

VI

Has This Happened Before?

The Great Depression and the Great Recession were both caused by policies derived from nostalgia for the world of the Enlighten- ment. Drawing on theories from the eighteenth century, hard- headed policy-makers either assumed or tried to re-create the idealized conditions described by Hume and Smith.

—Peter Temin (2010)

The argument up to now is that the rise of income inequality beginning around the mid-1970s brought on a decline in saving (and thus a rising APC) and eventually a surge in borrowing by households. The surge in borrowing was prompted by demand-side forces (stagnant household income and perceived wealth enhance- ment because of the housing bubble) and supply-side forces (relaxation of credit standards and low interest rates). With the bursting of the housing price bubble, the financial sys- tem almost collapsed, foreclosures ensued, many mortgage borrowers owed more than the value of their properties, and credit conditions were tightened by lenders even though interest rates remained low. The outcome to date is that households are deleveraging through saving more, borrowing less, and thus curbing their consumption. The rate of growth of real personal consumption expenditures since the official end of the Great Recession in the second quarter of 2009 through the fourth quarter of 2013 is a little over 2 percent per year. That compares with consumption growth averaging near 4 percent annually during the 1980s and 1990s. If deleveraging continues for some years, economic growth will be curtailed.

Has rising income inequality or rising household debt or a housing price bubble played a role in serious economic decline in the past? Did a rising average propensity to consume, and thus a falling rate of saving, warn of unsustainable consumption leading to a serious economic decline before the present recession? Those are the questions considered in this chapter, and they all receive the same answer: yes.

Rising Income Inequality in the 1920s

According to Marriner Eccles, U.S. Treasury Secretary during the Roosevelt administration, one cause of the Great Depression was income inequality because it led to an unsustainable rise of debt. "The stimulation to spending by debt-creation of this sort was short-lived and could not be counted on to sustain high levels of employment for long periods of time. Had there been a better distribution of the current income from the national product . . . we should have had far greater stability in our economy."[1] He wrote those words around 1951, the year his autobiography (*Beckoning Frontiers*) was published. That is the thesis about the Great Recession laid out in the preceding chapters.

Eccles was not alone in naming income inequality as a cause of the Great Depression. In his 1954 book *The Great Crash,* John Kenneth Galbraith lists "five weaknesses [that] seem to have had an especially intimate bearing on the ensuing disaster." First on his list is the "bad distribution of income."[2] He recognized that high-income people were most directly affected by the financial crash of 1929 because they owned almost all of the financial wealth. From the peak in October 1929, the Dow-Jones industrial average plummeted more than 80 percent to its low in late 1932. With so many investors' financial assets wiped out, their major cutbacks in spending spilled down to adversely affect lower-income households.

Table 6.1 presents three estimates of income shares from 1917 through 1939. The first two (Piketty and Saez, Kuznets) show the share of the bottom 95 percent, while the third (National Industrial Conference Board [NICB]) shows the share of the bottom 90 percent. Both the Piketty and Saez series and the Kuznets series show shares for every year from 1917 through 1939. In both series, 1920 is the peak year of income share for the bottom 95 percent for all years shown. Thereafter the share of the bottom 95 percent mostly declines, hitting a low of 65.2 percent in 1928 (Piketty and Saez) and 73.2 percent also in 1928 (Kuznets). The drop from the peak in 1920 is 7.3 percentage points in the Piketty and Saez series and a smaller 4.7 percentage points drop in the Kuznets series. Thereafter both series rise, but not steadily, through 1939. The point emphasized here is that there was a significant rise of income inequality in the 1920s—that is, the share of income going to the bottom 95 percent dropped from seven to five percentage points from 1920 to 1928.

The NICB series for selected years shows a different pattern. The peak share for the bottom 90 percent is 65.5 percent

Table 6.1. Income[a] Distribution, 1917–1939, Three Sources

Selected years	Piketty & Saez Bottom 95%	Kuznets Bottom 95%	NICB Bottom 90%
1917	69.7	75.4	
1918	70.7	77.3	65.5
1919	70.7	77.1	
1920	72.5	77.9	
1921	69.5	74.5	61.8
1922	69.0	75.2	
1923	71.1	77.1	
1924	69.1	75.7	
1925	67.5	74.8	
1926	67.3	74.8	
1927	66.6	74.0	
1928	65.2	73.2	
1929	67.0	73.9	61.0
1930	68.8	73.8	
1931	67.0	73.7	
1932	67.4	73.3	
1933	67.5	74.7	
1934	67.0	75.1	66.4
1935	69.0	76.3	
1936	67.4	75.7	
1937	68.6	76.2	65.6
1938	69.8	77.0	
1939	68.7	77.2	

[a] Excludes capital gains.

Sources: Alvaredo, Atkinson, Piketty, and Saez (2011); Kuznets (1946); U.S. Census Bureau (1975), series G337–352, and series A176–194, p. 302; National Industrial Conference Board (1949), Series A176–194, p. 15.

in 1918. Thereafter it is lower through 1929. Thus the NICB series agrees in direction of change with the other two series, falling almost five percentage points from 1918 to 1929. But the NICB drop in share, 1921–29, is less than one percentage point. By 1934 the NICB share is higher than its value in 1918: 65.5 percent. Yet all three series show increases of inequality in the 1920s, although slight in the NICB data.

But the rise of income inequality from 1920 to 1928, documented by Kuznets, was not noted by Friedman.[3] The Kuznets data on income distribution matches pretty well the data on income distribution assembled by Piketty, Saez, and colleagues from income tax returns for the period 1917–2002.[4]

In a paper on income inequality and poverty in the twentieth century, Eugene Smolensky and Robert Plotnick cite Jeffrey Williamson and Peter Lindert, who utilized the Kuznets data, income tax data, and skilled–unskilled wage ratios.[5] "The chronology of income inequality suggested by this assortment of time series is as follows. From the turn of the century until World War I, inequality was higher than in the latter half of the century. The war had a brief equalizing effect. Starting about 1920 inequality began to rise, reaching its pre–World War I level by 1929. From 1929 through 1951, inequality fell substantially."[6] The data of Table 6.1 and the observations by Smolensky and Plotkin about the analysis by Williamson and Lindert are in part at odds with the view of the labor economists Claudia Goldin and Lawrence Katz, who find "that the wage structure and the returns to education and skill all moved in the direction of greater equality considerably before the better known 'Great Compression' of the 1940s. The wage structure narrowed, skill differentials were reduced, and the return to education decreased sometime between 1890 and 1940, most likely in the late 1910s."[7] The part that is at odds with the data of Table 6.1 and the earlier studies cited above is that the "Great Compression" began "most likely in the late 1910s." But Table 6.1 shows that income inequality rose for parts of that period, 1920–28, according to the Piketty and Saez or the Kuznets series, and 1910–29 for the NICB series. Further, the description by Smolensky and Plotnick of Williamson's and Lindert's analysis claims that "starting about 1920 inequality began to rise, reaching its pre–World War I level by 1929."[8] The evidence shows that the turnaround from rising inequality to falling inequality did not begin until the 1930s.

Most of the analysis by Goldin and Katz relates to wage ratios for skilled and unskilled labor or professionals compared with manufacturing workers. It is true that their data on male workers' wage ratios in manufacturing for two years, 1890 and 1940, by various industries, show wage compression. However, their annual earnings ratios of college professors to average workers in manufacturing and average low-skilled workers in manufacturing for each year from 1908 to 1960 present a picture consistent with the data on income shares in Table 6.1. That is, although the ratios drop dramatically from 1908 to 1920, they then rise from 1920 through 1932. In some cases, the ratios of professors' earnings to those of low-skilled manufacturing workers were higher in 1932 than in 1908. The earnings ratios for all clerical workers, females, and production workers in manufacturing do not show as sharp a reversal of trend in the 1920s as with the professors.

Turning to income shares rather than earnings ratios, Goldin and Katz note, based on the Kuznets data and Goldsmith's 1967 and 1954 extensions, that "the share of income received by the top 5 percent of families (consumer units) declined from 30.0 percent in 1929 to 25.8 percent in 1939 to 20.9 percent in 1947. The important point here is that the Kuznets series does *not* rise during the 1930s. Rather the top portion of the income distribution narrowed during the Great Depression. The Kuznets data, therefore, reveal nothing particularly unusual about the late 1930s in comparison with the 1920s."[9] This quote agrees with the data presented in Table 6.1, except for the last sentence. As noted above, the three income share series presented in Table 6.1 show a declining share of income for the bottom 95 or 90 percent (thus a rising share for the top 5 or 10 percent) in the 1920s. That trend is reversed beginning in the early 1930s. Thus there is something noteworthy about the 1930s compared with the 1920s—namely, income inequality rose in the 1920s and began to fall in the 1930s.

The scenario of rising inequality in the 1920s followed by declining inequality in the 1930s and beyond is noted by Margo in his review of the inequality analysis by Williamson and Lindert. "Wage inequality drifted upwards after 1860, peaking at some point in the late 1920s, after experiencing a sharp, but transitory, decline during World War One. Inequality fell sharply and more or less continuously between 1929 and 1950."[10]

One likely reason for the sharp but short-lived drop of income inequality brought on by World War I is that agricultural prices exploded upward, a typical wartime phenomena. From a prewar wholesale price index (1967 = 100) of 43.7 in 1913, it shot up to a peak of 96.4 in 1919. The agricultural sector was far more important for the U.S. economy back then, accounting for 23 percent of national income and 27 percent of total employment in 1919. The average monthly wage for farm labor rose 141 percent from 1910 to 1920. But the end of the war and a national recession in the early 1920s brought on a collapse in agriculture. National income from agriculture plummeted 45 percent in only three years—1919 to 1922. The wholesale price index for farm products dropped 40 percent in that period, and the average monthly farm wage fell more than one-third.[11] With farm employment hardly changed in those three years, the effect on farm family annual incomes must have been severe. And given the relatively large size of the farm sector back then, the rising trend of income inequality from 1920 to 1929, shown in Table 6.1, is hardly surprising. Another piece of evidence supporting rising income inequality in the 1920s is the reversal of long-run state income convergence shown by Barro and Sala-i-Martin. Their measure of dispersion among states' per capita incomes, after declining from 1870 to 1920 (declines mean state incomes are growing closer together, as the neoclassical model predicts), turned up in the 1920s (rises mean state incomes are growing further apart, which can be a source of rising national income inequality, as noted in Chapter II).[12] It may not be a coincidence or an aberration that the shift from spatial convergence of state incomes to divergence, from the 1980s forward, includes a period of national rising income inequality, as does the 1920s.

But did the collapse in agriculture have a negative impact upon urban incomes, especially of the less skilled? Probably so, because migration of farm families to urban areas increased the supply of such labor. The net loss of farm population through migration was 6.3 million from 1920 to 1929. That is much higher than the net loss to migration in the 1930s of 3.8 million.[13]

The Long Rise of the Average Propensity to Consume

Simon Kuznets developed national income and consumption data for the United States back to 1869. In Table 6.2, what Kuznets calls "flow of goods to consumers" as a share of national income is labeled the APC because that is what he sought to measure in the early days of national income accounts. Those data are ten-year averages. In the three decades from 1884–93 to 1914–23, the APC rose 4.7 percentage points. In the next decade, it rose a further 5.4 percentage points. So the gain over four decades was ten percentage points, larger than the rise of almost seven percentage points from 1984 to the peak in 2005, shown in Figure 5.1 of Chapter V. Although the rise was larger, it took longer to develop. Nonetheless, the data for both periods contradict Friedman's argument that over the long run, the APC is stable.

"Estimates of savings in the United States made by Kuznets for the period since 1899 revealed no rise in the percentage of income saved over the past half-century despite a substantial rise in real income. According to his estimates, the percentage of income saved was much the same over the whole of the period."[14] It is true that the inferred saving rates, 1 – APC, of Kuznets in Table 6.2 show "no rise in the percentage of income saved over the past half-century," but they do show a *fall* in the saving rate from 16.1 percent in 1884–93 to 6.0 percent in 1924–33. Friedman does not note the specific ten-year APC estimates of Kuznets referred to above.

Friedman does show estimates of the APC by Raymond Goldsmith from time-series data for the United States for periods of varying length. The longest, 1897–1949, has an estimated APC of 0.88. All the shorter period estimates range from 0.87 to 0.89, except for one: 1929–41. For that period, estimated APC is 0.94, six points above the estimate for 1897–1949.[15] Note that the outlier in Kuznets's APC averages is for 1924–33, partly the same period, shown in Table 6.2. So the remarkable stability of Goldsmith's APCs must be qualified. If the APC is much above the long-term average for ten to thirteen years, then the saving rate was not "much the same over the whole period."[16]

Which estimates of the APC, Kuznets's or Goldsmith's, better agree with Friedman's assertion of stability? In order to compare them, from the annual data Goldsmith presents in his three-volume book *A Study of Saving in the United States* (1955), the APC values have been calculated for the years that correspond to Kuznets's ten-year periods in Table 6.2 and are shown as well. The point to take away from this is that the Goldsmith APC values do not show a steady long-term rise of the APC (and fall of the saving rate) from 1894–1903 through 1924–33. Rather, the Goldsmith figures show an APC rise over a shorter period: 1914–23 through 1924–33. Thus the Goldsmith figures that Friedman presented are more agreeable with Friedman's hypothesis of a constant saving rate and a stable APC than are the Kuznets figures.

Kuznets's data show a long period of rising APC in the first half of the twentieth century that also includes a period of rising income inequality. The current data show that income inequality has been rising for around thirty years (see Table 2.2) and that the APC has been rising for much of that same period—1984 to 2005. Kuznets's data show that income inequality rose from 1920 to 1928 (as do the Piketty and Saez data) and that the APC rose for the four decades after 1884–93. The fact that those two events overlap *twice* in our economic history may not be a coincidence. The rough temporal coincidence of rising APC and increasing income inequality for two long periods cannot be explained with Friedman's theory of consumption. Also, the rise of income inequality during 1920–28 shown in Table 6.1 was preceded by a long rise of income inequality briefly interrupted by World War I. That ear-

Table 6.2. Data on Average Propensity to Consume (APC) and Inferred Saving Rate, Kuznets (1874–1933) and Goldsmith (1897–1933)

Period	Kuznets		Goldsmith	
	Average APC	Inferred saving rate	Average APC	Inferred saving rate
1874–83	85.6%	14.4%	N/A	N/A
1884–93	83.9%	16.1%	N/A	N/A
1894–1903	85.2%	14.8%	90.9%[a]	9.1%[a]
1904–13	86.9%	13.1%	90.3%	9.7%
1914–23	88.6%	11.4%	88.1%	11.9%
1924–33	94.0%	6.0%	93.4%	6.6%

[a] 1897–1903

Source: Author's compilation from Kuznets (1946); APC averages from Table 16, p. 53. Inferred saving rate calculated as 1 – APC. Author's compilation from Goldsmith (1955): disposable income in current dollars (Vol. III, Table N–3, columns 7 and 8, p. 431) less personal saving in current dollars (Vol. I, Table T–6, columns 1–5) equals consumption in current dollars.

lier trend is documented by Williamson and Lindert. "Both measures [income tax data from top income groups] show peak inequalities on the eve of America's entry into World War I and again just before the Great Crash."[17]

The Rise of Household Debt

The evidence presented here shows that income inequality rose during the 1920s. Chapter IV argues that the huge run-up in household debt prior to the Great Recession was in part a response to rising inequality that depressed household income growth. Did debt rise during the 1920s? Yes. Figure 6.1 shows aggregate household debt to GDP for the period 1920–31. Figure

Figure 6.1. Debt to GDP ratio and share of top 5 percent in income distribution, 1920–31. *Sources:* Data for debt and GNP from U.S. Census Bureau (1975), tables on pp. 289 and 224. The share of top 5 percent in income distribution is from Saez (2013).

6.2 shows the same for the period 1983–2012. Figures 6.1 and 6.2 are duplicates of two graphs shown in "Inequality, Leverage and Crises: The Case of Endogenous Default" by Kumhof, Ranciere, and Winant. The authors note about this comparison:

> In the periods prior to both major crises, rapidly growing income inequality was accompanied by a

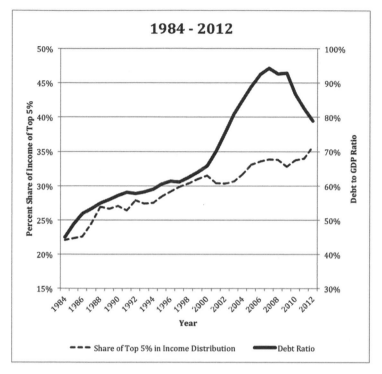

Figure 6.2. Debt to GDP ratio and share of top 5 percent in income distribution, 1984–2012. *Sources:* Debt is mortgage debt and consumer credit of households from Federal Reserve Board (2014a), Table L100. GDP is from Council of Economic Advisers (2013). Share of top 5 percent in income distribution is from Saez (2013).

sharp increase in aggregate household debt. . . . Between 1920 and 1928, the top 5% income share increased from 27.4% to 34.8%. During the same period, the ratio of household debt to GDP more than doubled. . . . Between 1983 and 2007 income inequality experienced a sharp increase as the share of total income commanded by the top 5% of the income distribution increased from 21.8% in 1983 to 33.8% in 2007.[18]

Two other IMF economists argue that the recent rise of income inequality in the United States is similar to such a rise in the 1920s. "In both cases there was a boom in the financial sector, poor people borrowed a lot, and a huge financial crisis ensued." And further, "The recent global economic crisis, with its roots in U.S. financial markets, may have resulted, in part at least, from the increase in inequality." Then they conclude, "It would be a big mistake to separate analyses of growth and income distribution."[19]

Another similarity is the trend in mortgage debt. Figure 6.3 shows residential mortgage debt outstanding from 1910 to 1934. Also shown is the price index of single-family houses for twenty-two cities, based on sales for the same period. In the ten years from 1910 to 1920, mortgage debt doubled, and in the next ten years, 1920 to 1930, it more than tripled. The year 1930 was the peak year for mortgage debt, reaching 30.2 billion. It was not until 1947 that the 1930 peak was surpassed.

House prices rose 38 percent from 1910 to 1920, slowing somewhat after that. They peaked in 1925, edged down more to 1927, and then post 1928 went into a freefall through 1933. The price level in 1934 was down to the 1914 level (Figure 6.3). As described by Hockett:

> When real estate prices leveled off and then began falling in 1928, however, short-term mortgages could no longer be refinanced in full. Again, things were much as they are today. Resultant forced sales and foreclosures, which reached the rate of over 1,000 per day once some 50 % of all home mort-

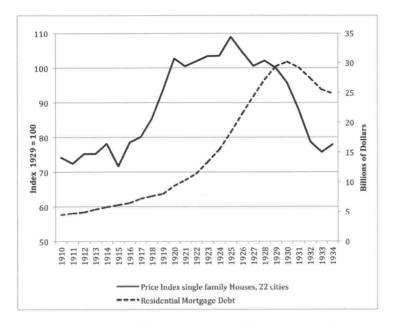

Figure 6.3. Mortgage debt outstanding and house prices, 1910–34.
The dashed line shows residential mortgage debt in billions of
dollars. Solid line: Price index of single family houses in twenty-two
cities. *Source:* U.S. Census Bureau (1975), House Price Indexes,
1890–1947, Series N 259–61; residential mortgage debt outstanding,
1890–1947, Series N 262–72.

gages in the country had gone into default, brought
prices steadily lower. The real estate market fell into
the familiar "downward spiral." The parallel with
today could not be more striking.[20]

As Hockett points out, one reason house prices fell so
much was that mortgage finance was rather short term in
the early part of the twentieth century, with down payments
typically more than 50 percent of value. Once house prices

stopped soaring, many homeowners could not refinance, the usual way to extend one's payback period. The thirty-year fully amortized mortgage was in fact a development prompted by the 1920s real estate collapse. Both the final year of the Hoover administration and the Roosevelt New Deal were responsible for bringing stability to mortgage finance with such improvements.[21]

Figure 6.4 presents mortgage debt and house prices for the recent past, 1991 to 2012. The growth of mortgage debt accelerated post 1995 to the peak in 2007. However, that recent expansionary period was not as strong as the tripling of mortgage debt from 1920 to 1930, shown in Figure 6.3. The rise of house prices was more rapid in the 1990s and 2000s than it was during the 1910 to 1925 period. The run-up of mortgage debt is greater in the earlier period, whereas the rise of house prices before the Great Depression was less sharp. Nonetheless, with 50 percent of all mortgages in the nation in default,[22] the real estate market collapse back then resembles the recent burst of the housing price bubble.

Non-mortgage consumer debt increased by a factor of two in the 1920s. Its peak of $7.6 million in 1929 was not exceeded for ten years thereafter. Although that seems a trivial amount, consumer credit terms were quite strict and default more costly for the debtor than today.[23] Krugman links income inequality to consumer debt in our current recession and speculates that "a return to pre-Depression levels of inequality . . . followed by a return to depression economics could be just a coincidence. Or it could reflect common causes of both phenomena."[24] After rejecting the underconsumption story of the current recession. Krugman argues, "A better case can be made for the opposite proposition—that rising inequality has led to too much consumption rather than too little and, more

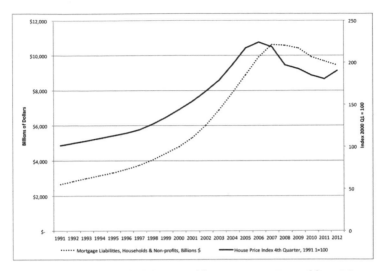

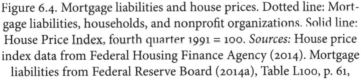

Figure 6.4. Mortgage liabilities and house prices. Dotted line: Mortgage liabilities, households, and nonprofit organizations. Solid line: House Price Index, fourth quarter 1991 = 100. *Sources:* House price index data from Federal Housing Finance Agency (2014). Mortgage liabilities from Federal Reserve Board (2014a), Table L100, p. 61, March 2014.

specifically, that the widening gaps in income have caused those left behind to take on too much debt."[25]

To what extent, then, was the period leading up to the Great Depression similar to that leading up to the Great Recession? They are similar in the rise of income inequality and in household debt, especially mortgage debt. It is true, though, that income inequality had been rising for more than thirty years in the current period before the debt burden brought down the economy in 2008, whereas income inequality had been rising for less than ten years when the debt burden contributed to the crash in 1929. The likely reason debt became unsustainable so much sooner in the 1920s is that credit conditions were far stricter back then.[26] The two periods are similar in the long-term rise of the APC and in the replacement of state income convergence with state income divergence. Also, the earlier period had a housing price bubble that burst in 1928.

Rising income inequality was a cause of rising household debt to unsustainable levels, which was an important factor in bringing on the Great Recession. As we have seen, rising income inequality in the 1920s was accompanied by rising mortgage debt. The regression results presented support the claim for the recent period. There is no statistical evidence linking rising income inequality to rising debt for the earlier period, but the historical evidence presented in this chapter does lend some support to the thesis of a causal link.

VII
Conclusion

It is clear that rising income inequality has had deleterious effects upon household debt and saving. The overhang of debt and revived saving by households post 2007 will be a drag on economic expansion for some years. The adverse aftereffects of the Great Recession, although officially ended in June 2009, will be much longer than those of recessions of the recent past. From the third quarter of 2009, the first quarter of official recovery from the Great Recession, through the fourth quarter of 2014, real consumption expenditures increased only 2.2 percent on average. That is well below the recent historical experience of nearly 4 percent.[1] Rather than conclude with views on how to jump-start or at least improve our limping economy, some authors are noted who have done a good job of prescribing policies for economic recovery. The book *The Way Forward: Moving from the Post-Bubble Post-Bust Economy to Renewed Growth and Competitiveness* (2011) by Daniel Alpert, Robert Hockett, and Nouriel Roubini lays out an impressive plan. Roubini was one of the few economists, Shiller another, who foresaw the financial crash. Paul Krugman's book *End This Depression Now!* (2012) also tells how to do it.[2] It is not rocket science. First-year students in macro-economics courses can design solutions. When unemployment is high, inflation is low, and interest rates near zero have no stimulative effect, it is clear that effective demand from consumers, businesses, and exporters is insufficient to restore full employment. Therefore the federal government must boost effective demand through deficit spending on massive infrastructure projects that have immediate and large employment effects. Tax cuts will not do in a high unemployment scenario because the unemployed are not paying any taxes, and so they gain no spending power. Those that do gain from tax cuts might save some or all, fearing times will get worse, or they might spend some of the first-round stimulus on imports. That will not help near-term recovery much.

In addition to telling how to bring on economic recovery, Krugman explains why a big short-term deficit to finance expansion of effective demand will *not* raise the long-term debt nearly as much as an austerity program such as the one imposed in the United Kingdom. That is because the rise of federal tax revenues in a full economic recovery can offset the deficit's effect on debt. We should have learned that after World War II. The heavy wartime borrowing by the government pushed the debt well above GDP, but the postwar economic boom brought the debt back down below GDP. The absolute debt may not have changed much, but its burden on the economy was reduced. He rightly labels inflation as "the phantom menace."[3] What faces us now is a higher danger of deflation than of inflation in such a slack economy.

Going beyond an easy-to-design short-term recovery program, the more daunting issue is how to reverse or at least stop the decades-long rise of income inequality, which, as argued here, has been a major cause of the Great Recession and our sluggish recovery. One thing is clear: the cause is mostly not economic—it is mostly political. So the solution, if ever devised, will be mostly political. Another financial and economic crash just as bad or worse than the last might focus Congress on correcting causes of income inequality.

The emphasis now is on what is new here. As noted in the Introduction and in Chapter V, the mainstream theory of consumption does not accord any importance to the distribution of income. But that theory cannot explain recent trends in relative consumption and saving. This analysis shows that rising income inequality was central to what has happened to relative consumption (the long-term rise of the APC) and consumer indebtedness. The state panel regressions of Chapter IV show that household debt rose with rising income inequality. The income quintile panel regressions show that the net change in household liabilities is positively related to increases of income inequality. The Consumer Expenditure Survey data show large gains in the relative share of consumer spending on shelter, health, and education while the share of non-housing necessities shrank. That is the case across all income quintiles. As argued in Chapter V, a revised theory of consumption should be developed that affords a central place to income distribution and household debt as well as to Modigliani and Brumberg's wealth-to-income ratio and to the persuasive insights of behavioral economics. To many, historical evidence carries more weight than econometric results, and to them, the evidence presented in Chapter VI may be the most persuasive evidence that rising income inequality can lead to unsustainable household debt that brings on a severe economic crash. The year 2008 looks like 1929.

Finally, I present a plea for a more fact-based economics than an authority-based economics. In the 1960s, when it became clear that indeed the APC, and of course the saving rate, were stable despite rapid income growth, Keynes's concern that income growth would lower the APC (and thus raise the saving rate) was jettisoned by macroeconomists. That was the right choice, and it was based on evidence. Starting in the mid-1980s, the APC began its long-term rise (and thus the long-term fall in the saving rate), which continued for twenty years. In the 2013 edition of his popular economics text, Gregory Mankiw argues that the APC in Friedman's consumption model will rise only "when current income temporarily falls below permanent income," as quoted in Chapter V. He also argues that the APC in Modigliani and Brumberg's consumption model will be constant because the wealth-to-income ratio will be constant over "long periods of time," also quoted in Chapter V. So although the actual APC has been rising for twenty years, a period no one would consider temporary, Mankiw explains why the APCs of the major authorities on the theory of consumption will be constant or at least stable. "Hence, in long-time series, one should observe a constant average propensity to consume, as in fact Kuznets found."[4] Did he look at the data? Why have today's economists failed to jettison the mainstream theory of consumption in the face of so much evidence to the contrary?

Notes

I
Introduction

1. Van Treeck (2012), p. 24.
2. Wolff (2010).
3. Stiglitz (2012); Rajan (2010); Krugman (2012); Palley (2012).
4. Cynamon and Fazzari (2013).
5. Piketty and Saez (2003, 2004).

II
Trends in Income Distribution

1. Information from 2009, calculated from Tables A0 and A1 at Piketty and Saez's web page, http://elsa.berkeley.edu/~saez/TabFig2007.xls.
2. Kaldor (1955–56).
3. Orszag (2011).
4. Stiglitz (2012), p. 64.
5. Stiglitz (2012), pp. 334–35.
6. Alvaredo, Atkinson, Piketty, and Saez (2011).
7. Palley (2002).
8. Dew-Becker and Gordon (2005), p. 125.
9. Horn et al. (2009).
10. Reich (2010).
11. Piketty and Saez (2003).
12. Barro and Sala-i-Martin (1991).
13. Drennan, Lobo, and Strumsky (2004).
14. James Galbraith (2012).

15. Alvaredo, Atkinson, Piketty, and Saez (2011).
16. Saez (2013).
17. Piketty and Saez (2004), p. 24.

III
Possible Causes of Rising Income Inequality

1. See Hacker and Pierson (2010); Kuttner (2007, 2013); Blank (2011); Johnson and Kwak (2011); Stiglitz (2012); Krugman (2012); Horn et al. (2009).
2. Piketty and Saez (2004).
3. Violante (2008), p. 520.
4. Blank (2011).
5. Mankiw (2013a).
6. Kaplan and Rauh (2013).
7. Dew-Becker and Gordon (2008), pp. 44–45.
8. Piketty and Saez (2003).
9. See Stiglitz (2012), p. 56; and Hacker and Pierson (2010).
10. Acemoglu and Autor (2011).
11. Mishel, Shierholz, and Schmitt (2013).
12. Piketty (2014).
13. Blank (2011).
14. Blank (2011), p. 12.
15. Blank (2011), p. 2.
16. DeNavas-Walt, Proctor, and Smith (2013).
17. Hacker and Pierson (2010).
18. Hacker and Pierson (2010), p. 187.
19. Hacker and Pierson (2010).
20. Hacker and Pierson (2010).
21. Stone (2010).
22. Hacker and Pierson (2010).
23. Hacker and Pierson (2010).
24. Hacker and Pierson (2010).
25. Drutman (2010).
26. Hacker and Pierson (2010).
27. Hacker and Pierson (2010).
28. Black (1997).
29. Stiglitz (2012), p. 35.
30. Mankiw (2013a), p. 23.
31. Stiglitz (2012), p. 37.
32. Gabaix and Landier (2006).

33. Dew-Becker and Gordon (2008), p. 45.

34. Bivins and Mishel (2013), Table 2.

IV
Consumers' Shift to Debt

1. See Boushey and Weller (2006); Dutt (2006); Hockett and Dillon (forthcoming); Mian and Sufi (2009a); van Treeck (2012); Kumhof, Ranciere, and Winant (2013); Reich (2010); Pollin (1988); Barba and Pivetti (2009); Horn et al. (2009); James Galbraith (2012); United Nations (2009); and IMF-ILO (2010).

2. Palumbo and Parker (2009).

3. Federal Reserve Board (2012).

4. Kumhof, Ranciere, and Winant (2013).

5. Mayer and Pence (2008).

6. Mian and Sufi (2009a).

7. Mayer and Pence (2008).

8. Mayer and Pence (2008), p. 2.

9. Federal Reserve Bank of New York (2011).

10. U.S. Courts (n.d.), "Bankruptcy Statistics."

11. Sullivan, Warren, and Westbrook (2006), p. 220.

12. Hockett and Dillon (forthcoming), p. 39.

13. Boushey and Weller (2006).

14. See Bureau of Labor Statistics (n.d.), "Consumer Expenditure Survey"; Garner, McClelland, and Passero (2009); and Passero (2009).

15. The Rockefeller Foundation (2010).

16. Communication by email with Jacob Hacker, creator of the Economic Security Index.

17. Stiglitz (2010b), p. 24.

18. See Carroll, Otsuka, and Slacalek (2011); Dynan (2009); and Mian and Sufi (2010).

19. See "The Long Climb" (2009); "From Ozzie to Ricky" (2009); and Rajan (2010).

20. Stiglitz (2010a), p. 4.

21. See Federal Reserve Board (2014b) and Shiller (2011).

22. Shiller (2011).

23. Mian and Sufi (2009b), pp. 1–2.

24. See Mian and Sufi (2009b), p. 3; Federal Reserve Board (2012); and M. Brown et al. (2013).

25. Mian and Sufi (2009b), p. 4.

26. Mian and Sufi (2009b), Abstract.

27. Wolff (2010), p. 21.
28. Wolff (2010), p. 22.

V

Consumption Theory and Its Critics

1. Varian (1990), p. 18.
2. Varian (1990), p. 295.
3. Kuznets (1955).
4. Okun (1975).
5. Krugman (2014).
6. Newman, Gayar, and Spencer (1954), pp. 158, 160, 163.
7. Schumpeter (1954).
8. Cottrell (1998).
9. Schumpeter (1954), p. 622.
10. Keynes (1951), pp. 113, 115–16.
11. Keynes (1951), p. 119.
12. Keynes (1951), p. 121.
13. Keynes (1951), p. 123.
14. Cottrell (1998), p. 63.
15. Keynes quoted in C. Brown (2004, p. 293).
16. See C. Brown (2004), p. 293, note 4.
17. Kuznets (1946).
18. Modigliani and Brumberg (1954).
19. Mankiw (2013b), p. 479.
20. Mankiw (2013b), p. 479.
21. Friedman (1957).
22. Mankiw (2013b), p. 483.
23. Friedman (1957), p. 18.
24. Friedman (1957), p. 19.
25. Hoover (2003), p. 425.
26. Krusell and Smith (1998), p. 890.
27. Friedman (1957), pp. 224–25.
28. Friedman (1957), p. 224.
29. Krueger and Perri (2006), p. 186.
30. Krueger and Perri (2006), p. 187.
31. Krueger and Perri (2006), p. 164.
32. Van Treeck (2012), p. 9.
33. Kopczuk, Saez, and Song (2010), p. 125.
34. Iacoviello (2008), pp. 929, 957.

35. See Frank and Levine (2005); Frank (2007); Barba and Pivetti (2009); Palley (2010); and Van Treeck (2012).

36. See Dynan, Skinner, and Zeldes (2004); Frank (2007); and Stiglitz (2012).

37. Kopczuk, Saez, and Song (2010), p. 125.

38. See Cynamon and Fazzari (2008), p. 25; and Pollin (1988).

39. Zellner (1960).

40. Rajan (2010), p. 42.

41. Van Treeck (2012), pp. 1–2. Van Treeck references Duesenberry (1949), Frank (1985), and Frank and Levine (2005).

42. Van Treeck (2012), p. 4.

43. Bordo and Meissner (2012), p. 1; Rajan (2010); Kumhof, Ranciere, and Winant (2013).

44. Malinen (2013), p. 2.

45. Malinen (2013), p. 13.

46. C. Brown (2004), p. 299.

47. C. Brown (2004), p. 303.

48. Bunting (2009), p. 293.

49. Bunting (2001), pp. 157–58.

50. See Veblen (1934, 1965).

51. Chase (1934).

52. Schumpeter (1954).

53. Bowles and Park (2004), p. 21.

54. Veblen (1898), p. 1.

55. Frank (2011), p. 17.

56. Bergstrom (2012).

57. Veblen (1898).

58. Duesenberry (1949), p. 26.

59. See Duesenberry (1949), quotes on pp. 28, 34, 101, 40, 45, 111–12, respectively.

60. Frank (1985), p. 37.

61. Luttmer (2005), p. 990.

62. Frank and Levine (2005), pp. 2, 3.

63. Frank (2007), pp. 75–76.

64. Akerlof (2002), p. 411.

65. Akerlof (2002), p. 412, 428.

66. Friedman (1957), p. 40.

67. Klyuev and Mills (2006).

68. See Cook (2005); also Tsionas and Christopoulos (2002).

69. See Krueger and Perri (2006); C. Brown (2004); and Iacoviello (2008).

70. Rajan (2010).

VI

Has This Happened Before?

1. Eccles (1951), p. 77.
2. John Kenneth Galbraith (1954), p. 182.
3. Kuznets (1946); Friedman (1957).
4. Alvaredo, Atkinson, Piketty, and Saez (2011).
5. Williamson and Lindert (1980).
6. Smolensky and Plotnick (1993), pp. 7–8.
7. Goldin and Katz (n.d.), pp. 25–26.
8. Smolensky and Plotnick (1993), p. 8.
9. Goldin and Katz (n.d.), pp. 4–5.
10. Margo (1999), p. 2.
11. National Industrial Conference Board (1949).
12. Barro and Sala-i-Martin (1991).
13. National Industrial Conference Board (1949).
14. Friedman (1957), pp. 3–4.
15. Friedman (1957), p. 126.
16. Friedman (1957), p. 4.
17. Williamson and Lindert (1980), p. 77.
18. Kumhof, Ranciere, and Winant (2013), pp. 9–10.
19. Berg and Ostry (2011), p. 13.
20. Hockett (2010), p. 1268.
21. Hockett (2010).
22. Hockett (2010).
23. Olney (1999).
24. Krugman (2012), p. 83.
25. Krugman (2012), pp. 83–84.
26. Olney (1999).

VII

Conclusion

1. Bureau of Economic Analysis (n.d.), Table 2.3.1.
2. Alpert, Hockett, and Roubini (2011); Krugman (2012).
3. Krugman (2009).
4. Mankiw (2013b), p. 483.

Bibliography

Acemoglu, Daron, and David Autor. 2011. "Skill Tasks and Technologies: Implications for Employment Earnings." In O. Ashenfelter and D. Card, eds., *The Handbook of Labor Economics*, vol. 4b. Amsterdam: Elsevier.

Akerlof, George. 2002. "Behavioral Macroeconomics and Macroeconomic Behavior." *American Economic Review* 923:411–33.

Alpert, Daniel, Robert Hockett, and Nouriel Roubini. 2011. *The Way Forward: Moving from the Post-Bubble Post-Bust Economy to Renewed Growth and Competitiveness*. New York: The New America Foundation.

Alvaredo, Facundo, Tony Atkinson, Thomas Piketty, and Emmanuel Saez. 2011. The World Top Incomes Database. http://topincomes.parisschool ofeconomics.eu/#Home.

Barba, Aldo, and Massimo Pivetti. 2009. "Rising Household Debt: Its Causes and Microeconomic Implications—a Long Period Analysis." *Cambridge Journal of Economics* 53:113–37.

Barro, Robert J., and Xavier Sala-i-Martin. 1991. "Convergence Across States and Regions." *Brookings Papers on Economic Activity* 1.

Berg, Andrew, and Jonathan Ostry. 2011. "Inequality and Unsustainable Growth: Two Sides of the Same Coin?" International Monetary Fund Staff Discussion Note.

Bergstrom, Ted. 2012. Review of Robert Frank's "The Darwin Economy: Liberty, Competition, and the Common Good." *Journal of Economic Literature* 503:795.

Bivins, Josh, and Lawrence Mishel. 2013. "The Pay of Corporate Executives and Financial Professionals as Evidence of Rents in Top 1 Percent Incomes." *Journal of Economic Perspectives* 273:57–78.

Black, John, ed. 1997. *Oxford Dictionary of Economics*. Oxford: Oxford University Press.

Blank, Rebecca M. 2011. *Changing Inequality.* Berkeley: University of California Press.

Bordo, Michael D., and Christopher M. Meissner. 2012. "Does Inequality Lead to Financial Crisis?" NBER Working Paper No. 17896.

Boushey, Heather, and Christian E. Weller. 2006. "Inequality and Household Economic Hardship in the United States of America." DESA Working Paper No. 18, U.N. Department of Economic & Social Affairs, pp. 1–26.

Bowles, Samuel, and Yongjin Park. 2004. "Emulation, Inequality, and Work Hours: Was Thorstein Veblen Right?" *Economic Journal* 115507:F397–F412.

Brown, Christopher. 2004. "Does Income Distribution Matter for Effective Demand? Evidence from the United States." *Review of Political Economy* 163:291–307.

Brown, Meta, Andrew Haughwout, Donghoon Lee, and Wilbert van der Klaauw. 2013. "The Financial Crisis at the Kitchen Table: Trends in Household Debt and Credit." *Current Issues in Economics and Finance* 19(2):1–10.

Bunting, David. 2001. "Keynes' Law and Its Critics." *Journal of Post Keynesian Economics* 241:149–63.

———. 2009. "The Saving Decline: Macro-Facts, Micro-Behavior." *Journal of Economic Behavior & Organization* 701–2:282–95.

Bureau of Economic Analysis, U.S. Department of Commerce. n.d. "Gross Domestic Product." Available at http://www.bea.gov/national/index.htm#gdp.

———. n.d. "National Economic Accounts." http://www.bea.gov/national/index.htm.

———. n.d. "Table 2.3.1. Percent Change from Preceding Period in Real Personal Consumption Expenditures by Major Type of Product." Available at http://www.bea.gov/national/index.htm#personal.

———. n.d. "Table S.3.a. Households and Nonprofit Institutions Serving Households." Available at http://www.bea.gov/national/nipaweb/NI_FedBeaSna/Index.asp.

Bureau of Labor Statistics, U.S. Department of Labor. n.d. "Consumer Expenditure Survey, 1984–2010." http://www.bls.gov/cex/#tables.

———. n.d. "Consumer Price Index." http://www.bls.gov/cpi.

———. 2015. "News Release, Productivity and Costs" [press release], March 5.

Carroll, Christopher D., Misuzu Otsuka, and Jiri Slacalek. 2011. "How Large Are Housing and Financial Wealth Effects? A New Approach." *Journal of Money, Credit, and Banking* 431:55–79.

Case-Shiller House Price Index. 2012. http://www.econ.yale.edu/~shiller/data.htm.

Chase, Stuart. 1934. Foreword to *Theory of the Leisure Class*. New York: Modern Library.

Cook, Steven. 2005. "The Stationarity of Consumption-Income Ratios: Evidence from Minimum LM Unit Root Testing." *Economics Letters* 89:55–60.

Cottrell, A. 1998. "Keynes, Ricardo, Malthus and Say's Law." In James Ahrakpor, ed., *Keynes and the Classics Reconsidered*, pp. 63–75. Boston: Kluwer Academic.

Council of Economic Advisers. 2011. *Economic Report of the President*. Washington, DC: U.S. Government Printing Office.

———. 2013. *Economic Report of the President*. Washington, DC: U.S. Government Printing Office.

Cynamon, Barry, and Steven M. Fazzari. 2008. "Household Debt in the Consumer Age: Source of Growth—Risk of Collapse." *Capitalism and Society* 3(2):1–30.

———. 2013. "Inequality, the Great Recession, and a Stagnant Recovery." http://www.eaepeparis2013.com/papers/Full_Paper_Barry-Cynamon -Fazzari.pdf.

DeNavas-Walt, Carmen, and Bernadette D. Proctor, U.S. Census Bureau. 2014. *Income, Poverty, and Health Insurance Coverage in the United States: 2013*. Current Population Reports, P60-249. Washington, DC: U.S. Government Printing Office. http://www.census.gov/content/dam/ Census/library/publications/2014/demo/p60-249.pdf.

DeNavas-Walt, Carmen, Bernadette D. Proctor, and Jessica C. Smith, U.S. Census Bureau. 2011. *Income, Poverty, and Health Insurance Coverage in the United States: 2010*. Current Population Reports, P60-239. Washington, DC: U.S. Government Printing Office. http://www.census .gov/prod/2011pubs/p60-239.pdf.

———. 2013. *Income, Poverty, and Health Insurance Coverage in the United States: 2012*. Current Population Reports, P60-245. Washington, DC: U.S. Government Printing Office. http://www.census.gov/prod/2013 pubs/p60-245.pdf.

Dew-Becker, Ian, and Robert J. Gordon. 2005. "Where Did the Productivity Growth Go? Inflation Dynamics and the Distribution of Income." *Brookings Papers on Economic Activity* 2:67–122.

———. 2008. "Controversies About the Rise of American Inequality: A Survey." NBER Working Paper Submission, April 21.

Drennan, Matthew P., Jose Lobo, and Deborah Strumsky. 2004. "Unit Root Tests of Sigma Income Convergence Across US Metropolitan Areas." *Journal of Economic Geography* 4(5):583–95.

Drutman, Lee Jared. 2010. "The Business of America Is Lobbying: The Expansion of Corporate Political Activity and the Future of American Pluralism." Ph.D. dissertation, University of California, Berkeley.

Duesenberry, James S. 1949. *Income, Saving and the Theory of Consumer Behavior.* Cambridge, MA: Harvard University Press.

Dutt, Amitav K. 2006. "Maturity, Stagnation and Consumer Debt: A Steindlian Approach." *Metroeconomica* 57(3):339–64.

Dynan, Karen E. 2009. "Changing Household Financing Opportunities and Economic Security." *Journal of Economic Perspectives* 23(4):49–68.

Dynan, Karen E., Jonathan Skinner, and Stephen Zeldes. 2004. "Do the Rich Save More?" *Journal of Political Economy* 112(2):397–442.

Eccles, Marriner. 1951. *Beckoning Frontiers.* New York: Alfred A. Knopf.

Federal Housing Finance Agency. 2014. House Price Index. http://www.fhfa .gov/DataTools/Downloads/Pages/House-Price-Index.aspx.

Federal Reserve Bank of New York. 2011. "Household Debt and Credit." August.

Federal Reserve Board. 2009. "Survey of Consumer Finances, 2007." http:// www.federalreserve.gov/pubs/oss/oss2/2007/scf2007home.html.

———. 2012. "Survey of Consumer Finances, 2010." http://www.federalreserve .gov/econresdata/scf/scf_2010.htm.

———. 2014a. *Financial Accounts of the United States: Flow of Funds, Balance Sheets, and Integrated Macroeconomic Accounts—Historical Annual Tables, 2005–2013.* http://www.federalreserve.gov/releases/z1/Current/annuals/ a2005-2013.pdf.

———. 2014b. "Household Debt Service and Financial Obligations Ratios." http://www.federalreserve.gov/datadownload/Download.aspx?rel=FOR &series=767f957af5d4d8e28f95408bfb53e557&filetype=spreadsheetml&la bel=include&layout=seriescolumn&from=03/01/1980&to=03/31/2014.

Frank, Robert H. 1985. *Choosing the Right Pond.* New York: Oxford University Press.

———. 2007. *Falling Behind.* Berkeley: University of California Press.

———. 2011. *The Darwin Economy: Liberty, Competition, and the Common Good.* Princeton, NJ: Princeton University Press.

Frank, Robert H., and Seth Levine. 2005. "Expenditure Cascades." https:// www.aeaweb.org/annual_mtg_papers/2007/0107_1300_0202.pdf.

Friedman, Milton. 1957. *A Theory of the Consumption Function.* National Bureau of Economic Research. Princeton, NJ: Princeton University Press.

"From Ozzie to Ricky." 2009. *Economist,* October 3–9, pp. 5–8.

Gabaix, Xavier, and Augustin Landier. 2006. "Why Has CEO PAY Increased So Much?" *Quarterly Journal of Economics* 123(1):49–100.

Galbraith, James. 2012. *Inequality and Instability.* Oxford: Oxford University Press.

Galbraith, John Kenneth. 1954. *The Great Crash*. New York: Houghton Mifflin.

Garner, Thesia I., Robert McClelland, and William Passero. 2009. "Strengths and Weaknesses of the Consumer Expenditure Survey from a BLS Perspective." NBER Summer Institute, Conference on Research on Income and Wealth, Cambridge, Massachusetts, July 13.

Goldin, Claudia, and Lawrence F. Katz. n.d., n.p. "Decreasing and Then Increasing Inequality in America: A Tale of Two Half-Centuries."

Goldsmith, Raymond W. 1955. *A Study of Saving in the United States*. 3 vols. Princeton, NJ: Princeton University Press.

Hacker, Jacob S. 2015. Economic Security Index. http://www.economicsecurityindex.org/?p=home.

Hacker, Jacob S., and Paul Pierson. 2010. "Winner-Take-All Politics: Public Policy, Political Organization, and the Precipitous Rise of Top Incomes in the United States." *Politics and Society* 38(2):152–204.

Hockett, Robert. 2010. "A Fixer-Upper for Finance." *Washington University Law Review* 87(6):1213–91.

Hockett, Robert, and Daniel Dillon. Forthcoming. "Income Inequality and Market Fragility: Some Empirics in the Political Economy of Finance." *Northeastern Economic Journal*.

Hoover, Kevin D. 2003. "A History of Postwar Monetary Economics and Macroeconomics." In Warren J. Samuels, Jeff E. Biddle, and John B. Davis, eds., *A Companion to the History of Economic Thought*, pp. 411–27. Oxford: Blackwell.

Horn, Gustav, Katharina Droge, Simon Sturn, Till van Treeck, and Rudolph Zweiner. 2009. "From the Financial Crisis to the World Economic Crisis: The Role of Inequality." IMK Report No. 41, Policy Brief.

Iacoviello, Matteo. 2008. "Household Debt and Income Inequality." *Journal of Money, Credit and Banking* 40(5):929–65.

IMF-ILO. 2010. "The Challenges of Growth, Employment and Social Cohesion." Proceedings from joint IMF-ILO conference, Oslo, Norway, September 13.

Johnson, Simon, and James Kwak. 2011. *Thirteen Bankers*. New York: Random House.

Kaldor, Nicolas. 1955–56. "Alternative Theories of Distribution." *Review of Economic Studies* 23(2):83–100.

Kaplan, Steven N., and Joshua Rauh. 2013. "It's the Market: The Broad-Based Rise in the Return to Top Talent." *Journal of Economic Perspectives* 27(3):35–56.

Keynes, John Maynard. 1936. *The General Theory of Employment, Interest and Money*. London: Macmillan.

———. 1951. *Essays in Biography.* New York: Horizon Press.

Klyuev, Vladamir, and Paul Mills. 2006. "Is Housing Wealth an ATM? The Relationship Between Household Wealth, Home Equity Withdrawal and Saving Rates." International Monetary Fund Working Paper 06/162.

Kopczuk, Wojciech, Emmanuel Saez, and Jae Song. 2010. "Earnings Inequality and Mobility in the United States: Evidence from Social Security Data Since 1937." *Quarterly Journal of Economics* 125(1):91–128.

Krueger, Dirk, and Fabrizio Perri. 2006. "Does Income Inequality Lead to Consumption Inequality? Evidence and Theory." *Review of Economic Studies* 73:163–93.

Krugman, Paul. 2009. "Role Reversal." *New York Times,* November 22.

———. 2012. *End This Depression Now!* New York: W. W. Norton.

———. 2014. "Why We Are in a New Gilded Age." *New York Review of Books,* May 8.

Krusell, Per, and Anthony A. Smith, Jr. 1998. "Income and Wealth Heterogeneity in the Macroeconomy." *Journal of Political Economy* 106(5):867–96.

Kumhof, Michael, Romain Ranciere, and Pablo Winant. 2013. "Inequality, Leverage and Crises: The Case of Endogenous Default." International Monetary Fund Working Paper, WP/13/249.

Kuttner, Robert. 2007. *The Squandering of America: How the Failure of Our Politics Undermines Our Prosperity.* New York: Alfred A. Knopf.

———. 2013. *Debtors' Prison.* New York: Alfred A. Knopf.

Kuznets, Simon S. 1946. *National Income: A Summary of Findings.* New York: National Bureau of Economic Research.

———. 1955. "Economic Growth and Income Inequality." *American Economic Review* 45(1):1–28.

"The Long Climb." 2009. *Economist,* October 3–9, p. 8.

Luttmer, Erzo F. P. 2005. "Neighbors as Negatives: Relative Earnings and Well-Being." *Quarterly Journal of Economics,* August, pp. 963–1002.

Malinen, Tuomas. 2013. "Is There a Relationship Between Income Inequality and Leverage?" Helsinki Center of Economic Research, Discussion Paper No. 362.

Mankiw, N. Gregory. 2013a. "Defending the One Percent." *Journal of Economic Perspectives* 27(3):21–34.

———. 2013b. *Macroeconomics,* 8th edition. Houndmills, UK: Palgrave Macmillan.

Margo, Robert A. 1999. "The History of Wage Inequality in America, 1820 to 1970." Social Science Research Network, Working Paper No. 286.

Mayer, Christopher J., and Karen Pence. 2008. "Subprime Mortgages: What, Where, and to Whom?" NBER Working Paper 14083.

Mian, Atif, and Amir Sufi. 2009a. "The Consequences of Mortgage Credit Expansion: Evidence from the U.S. Mortgage Default Crisis." *Quarterly Journal of Economics*, November, pp. 1449–96.

———. 2009b. "House Prices, Home Equity-Based Borrowing, and the United States Household Leverage Crisis." National Bureau of Economic Research, Working Paper no. 15283.

———. 2010. "Household Leverage and the Recession of 2007 to 2009." NBER Working Paper, No. 15896.

Mishel, Lawrence, Heidi Shierholz, and John Schmitt. 2013. "Don't Blame the Robots: Assessing the Job Polarization Explanation of Growing Wage Inequality." Working Paper, Economic Policy Institute.

Modigliani, Franco, and Richard Brumberg. 1954. "Utility Analysis and the Consumption Function: An Interpretation of Cross-Section Data." In K. K. Kurihara, ed., *Post-Keynesian Economics*, pp. 3–45. New Brunswick, NJ: Rutgers University Press.

National Industrial Conference Board (NICB). 1949. "National Income–Percentage of Income Received by Specified Proportion of Recipients Arranged According to Size of Income: 1910 to 1937." In U.S. Census, *Historical Statistics of the United States, 1789–1945*, Series A 176–94. Washington, DC: U.S. Government Printing Office.

Newman, Philip C., Arthur D. Gayar, and Milton H. Spencer, eds. 1954. *Source Readings in Economic Thought*. New York: W. W. Norton.

Okun, Arthur M. 1975. *Equality and Efficiency: The Great Tradeoff*. Washington, DC: Brookings Institution.

Olney, Martha L. 1999. "Avoiding Default: The Role of Credit in the Consumption Collapse of 1930." *Quarterly Journal of Economics* 114(1):319–35.

Orszag, Peter. 2011. "As Kaldor's Facts Fall, Occupy Wall Street Rises." *Bloomberg View*, October 18.

Palley, Thomas I. 2002. "Economic Contradictions Coming Home to Roost? Does the U.S. Economy Face a Long-Term Aggregate Demand Generation Problem?" *Journal of Post Keynesian Economics* 25(1):9–32.

———. 2010. "The Relative Permanent Income Theory of Consumption: A Synthetic Keynes-Duesenberry-Friedman Model." *Review of Political Economy* 22(1):41–56.

———. 2012. *From Financial Crisis to Stagnation*. Cambridge: Cambridge University Press.

Palumbo, Michael J., and Jonathan A. Parker. 2009. "The Integrated Financial and Real System of National Accounts for the United States: Does It Presage the Financial Crisis?" NBER Working Paper 14663.

Passero, William. 2009. "The Impact of Income Imputation in the Consumer Expenditure Survey." *Monthly Labor Review,* August, pp. 25–42.

Piketty, Thomas. 2014. *Capital in the Twenty-first Century.* Cambridge, MA: Belknap Press of Harvard University Press.

Piketty, Thomas, and Emmanuel Saez. 2003. "Income Inequality in the United States, 1913–1998." *Quarterly Journal of Economics* 118(1):1–39.

———. 2004. "Income Inequality in the United States, 1913–2002." University of California, Berkeley, Department of Economics. http://elsa.berkeley .edu/~saez/piketty-saezOUP04US.pdf.

Pollin, Robert. 1988. "The Growth of U.S. Household Debt: Demand-Side Influences." *Journal of Macroeconomics* 10(2):231–48.

Rajan, Raghuram G. 2010. *Fault Lines: How Hidden Fractures Still Threaten the World Economy.* Princeton, NJ: Princeton University Press.

Reich, Robert B. 2010. *Aftershock.* New York: Vintage Books.

The Rockefeller Foundation. 2010. "More Americans Are Financially Insecure Now Than in the Past 25 Years." http://www.rockefellerfounda tion.org/news/publications/more-americans-are-financially-insecure.

Saez, Emanuel. 2013. "Striking It Richer: The Evolution of Top Income in the United States." *Pathways,* Winter 2008, 6–7; http://elsa.berkeley .edu/~saez/TabFig2012prel.xls.

Schumpeter, Joseph A. 1954. *History of Economic Analysis.* New York: Oxford University Press.

Shiller, Robert J. 2011. "The Sickness Beneath the Slump." *New York Times,* June 12.

Smolensky, Eugene, and Robert Plotnick. 1993. "Inequality and Poverty in the United States: 1900 to 1990." Institute for Research on Poverty, Discussion Paper #998–93.

Stiglitz, Joseph E. 2010a. *Free Fall.* New York: W. W. Norton.

———. 2010b. *The Stiglitz Report: Reforming the International Monetary and Financial Systems in the Wake of the Global Crisis.* New York: New Press.

———. 2012. *The Price of Inequality.* New York: W. W. Norton.

Stone, Katherine V. W. 2010. "John R. Commons and the Origins of Legal Realism, or the Other Tragedy of the Commons." In A. Brophy and D. Hamilton, eds., *Transformations in American Legal History,* vol. 2, pp. 326–43. Cambridge, MA: Harvard University Press.

Sullivan, Teresa A., Elizabeth Warren, and Jay Lawrence Westbrook. 2006. "Less Stigma or More Financial Distress: An Empirical Analysis of the

Extraordinary Increase in Bankruptcy Filings." *Stanford Law Review* 59(2):213–56.

Temin, Peter. 2010. "The Great Recession and the Great Depression." *Daedalus* 139(4):115–24.

Tsionas, Eftymios, and Dmitris Christopoulos. 2002. "Non-Stationarity in the Consumption-Income Ratio: Further Evidence from Panel and Asymmetric Unit Root Tests." *Economics Bulletin* 3(122):1–5.

United Nations. 2009. *Report of the Commission of Experts of the President of the United Nations General Assembly on Reforms of the International Monetary and Financial System.* New York: United Nations. http://www .un.org/ga/econcrisissummit/docs/FinalReport_CoE.pdf.

U.S. Census Bureau. 1975. *Historical Statistics of the United States, Colonial Times to 1970.* Washington, DC: U.S. Government Printing Office.

———. 2009. "Historical Income Tables—Households." http://www.census .gov/hhes/www/income/data/historical/household/index.html.

U.S. Courts. n.d. "Bankruptcy Statistics." http://www.uscourts.gov/Statistics /BankruptcyStatistics.aspx.

Van Treeck, Till. 2012. "Did Inequality Cause the U.S. Financial Crisis?" IMK Working Paper 91, pp. 1–39.

Varian, H. R. 1990. *Intermediate Microeconomics: A Modern Approach,* 2nd edition. New York: W. W. Norton.

Veblen, Thorstein. 1898. "Why Is Economics Not an Evolutionary Science." *Quarterly Journal of Economics* 12:2–17.

———. 1934. *The Theory of the Leisure Class.* New York: Modern Library.

———. 1965. *The Theory of Business Enterprise.* New York: A. M. Kelley.

Violante, Giovanni L. 2008. "Skill-Biased Technological Change." In *The New Palgrave Dictionary of Economics,* 2nd edition, ed. Steven N. Durlauf and Lawrence E. Blume. New York: Palgrave Macmillan.

Williamson, Jeffrey G., and Peter H. Lindert. 1980. *American Inequality: A Macroeconomic History.* New York: Academic Press.

Wolff, Edward N. 2010. "Recent Trends in Household Wealth in the United States: Rising Debt and the Middle-Class Squeeze—An Update to 2007." Levy Economics Institute, Working Paper No. 589.

Zellner, Arnold. 1960. "Tests of Some Basic Propositions in the Theory of Consumption." *American Economic Review* 50(2):565–73.

Index